Anna M. Tunstall

Salt in my Porridge

Adult Fiction

The Golden Venus Affair
Duel in Glenfinnan
Maniac
Night on the Killer Reef
The Canisbay Conspiracy
Murder at the Open
The Grey Shepherds
The Hammers of Fingal
The Killings on Kersivay
The Dancing Horse
Escort to Adventure
Fugitive's Road
Greybreek
Death on the Machar
The Crouching Spy
Strangers from the Sea
Eleven for Danger
The Singing Spider
Crime's Masquerader
The Crooked Finger
Flowering Death
The Cavern
The Ten Green Brothers
The Temple Falls
The Screaming Gull
Death by the Mistletoe
The Purple Rock

Children's Fiction

Super Nova and the Frozen Man
Super Nova and the Rogue Satellite
Life-boat—Green to White
The Cave of the Hammers
The Kersivay Kraken
The High Cliffs of Kersivay
Space Agent and the Ancient Peril
Space Agent and the Isles of Fire
Space Agent from the Lost Planet
Kilpatrick, Special Reporter
Satellite 7
The Atom Chasers in Tibet
The Atom Chasers
Dinny Smith Comes Home
Peril on the Lost Planet
Red Fire on the Lost Planet
Secret of the Lost Planet
Return to the Lost Planet
The Lost Planet
Tiger Mountain
The Grey Pilot
Stubby Sees It Through
King Abbie's Adventure
Faraway Island
The Black Wherry
The Crocodile Men

Plays

Minister's Monday
Stranger at Christmas
Final Proof
Mercy Flight
Storm Tide
Under Suspicion

Non-fiction

Rescue Call
Let's Visit Scotland

ANGUS MacVICAR

Salt
in my Porridge

CONFESSIONS OF A MINISTER'S SON

 JARROLDS, LONDON

JARROLDS PUBLISHERS (LONDON) LTD
3 Fitzroy Square, London W1

AN IMPRINT OF THE HUTCHINSON GROUP

London Melbourne Sydney Auckland
Wellington Johannesburg Cape Town
and agencies throughout the world

First published January 1971
Second impression February 1971
Third impression May 1971
Fourth impression October 1971
Fifth impression August 1972

Printed in Great Britain by litho on antique wove paper
by Anchor Press, Tiptree, Essex, and bound by
Leighton-Straker Bookbinding Co. Ltd, London

ISBN 0 09 105250 5

To
My Mother, Rona, Archie and Maimie
who no doubt are having a good laugh at the
antics of the MacVicars still alive

Acknowledgments

My grateful thanks are due to 'the Padre' for allowing me to quote from *Hebridean Heritage,* one of the three booklets he has published since his retirement, all now out of print; to Willie for making available his personal account of the desperate voyage of *Britannia's* Life-boat No. 7; to Kenneth for letting me use extracts from his own story of an exciting escape in Burma; and to the Rev. Ronald Falconer, DD, Head of Religious Broadcasting, Scotland, Mr Ian McColl, Editor of the *Scottish Daily Express,* Bill More of Campbeltown, the *Daily Record* and the Outram Press for their kind permission to reproduce photographs.

A.M.

Contents

Illustrations

I

The Bursting Boughs of May

In 1924, the year we poached a salmon for the Moderator, there were only five of us: myself, aged fifteen; Archie, twelve; Willie, ten; Rona, six, and Kenneth, a baby in his cot. John, the youngest, had yet to be born.

At the time, as minister of the small country parish of Southend, Kintyre, my father drew an annual stipend which fluctuated on the edge of £350, out of which he had to maintain a Manse with eleven rooms, six dilapidated outhouses and a garden like a park, as well as a hungry family. He had never heard of such a thing as an expense account. In the circumstances, a two-day visit of the Moderator of the Church of Scotland, touring Kintyre in mid-autumn, posed for him an anxious problem. On the administrative side it posed an even more anxious problem for my mother—and for Maimie, the maid.

The Moderator, however, turned out to be a jovial man— he was the Right Rev. David Cathels, DD, of Hawick— who could discuss not only Church Law but also other more interesting subjects: fishing and golf, for example, and the Olympic achievements of Eric Liddell. He complimented my mother on her soda scones, and when Rona upset her breakfast milk on his shiny black breeches, his infectious chuckle soon chased away visions of a wrath to come.

At about five o'clock on the second evening, disaster struck. By this time the chickens and eggs supplied by kindly parishioners had all been eaten, but as a special treat for our guest at what we called 'the last supper', my mother had reserved a magnificent cold tongue. For some reason, however, the larder door was left open, and Roy, a yellow collie from the neighbouring farm of Kilblaan, saw his chance and took it. The last anybody saw of the tongue was in Roy's mouth as he disappeared over the garden wall with a flick of his white-tipped tail.

Tears were in my mother's eyes. Though guiltless, for once, Archie and I stood by her, consumed by sympathy. Willie and Rona had gone to ground beneath gooseberry-bushes in the garden: a prudent move, because Maimie was darting back and forth, scolding everybody.

'Now all we have is tinned salmon!' said my mother. 'Think of it. Tinned salmon for the most important man in Scotland, next to the King!'

My father, always inept in a domestic crisis, muttered a vague 'Dominus providebit', which happens to be the motto of our clan. But Archie and I exchanged looks of inspiration. We went out into the garden and joined Willie and Rona under the gooseberries.

'Listen!' I said, with an eldest brother's authority. 'There's a big salmon in the pool below the bridge: we saw him this morning. If we caught him now, he could be cooked in time for supper.'

'Your rod's broke,' said Rona.

'I've thought of something else. We'll make a landing-net out of the Dutch-hoe, a loop of fence wire and the string net from Kenneth's cot.'

Archie, the honest one, said: 'That'll be poaching.'

'Yes, but it's for the Moderator. He's a holy man, so it's okay.'

Some years later, studying Moral Philosophy at Glasgow University, we both detected a flaw in this argument. But at the time it satisfied us; and when our preparations were complete we went into action with no qualms of conscience.

A latter-day Penelope, Rona remained at the Manse to counter awkward questions with guileless words; Archie and Willie took up their positions as scouts, a hundred yards away on either side of the bridge, while I, chewing a handful of gooseberries as a rather frightened gangster might chew gum, crept cautiously to the burn's edge.

I saw him at once in the clear water, brown, red-spotted, sensuously rubbing himself against a boulder. His nose pointed upstream; his tail moving from side to side.

Gripping a bridge support with one hand, I lowered the net with the other. In the evening quiet the only sound was a tinkle from the burn as it flowed steeply into the pool. Scent of newly cut corn mingled with a tarry odour from the bridge.

He saw the net and twitched backwards. I persisted, holding impatience in check. The white string bag moved towards him: eighteen inches, a foot, six inches. My mouth was dry and salty.

Then I decided to stake our plan on one desperate sweep. Tense with anticipation, I thrust the net forward and, as I thrust, suddenly found inside it a furious, fighting, twelve-pound fish. I tried to heave it up but lost my hold of the bridge support. I slipped and fell and splashed headlong into the water.

A shock of fair hair appeared above me. 'The keeper's coming!' said Archie.

I struggled out of the burn and killed the salmon with a stone. 'Act the decoy!' I ordered. 'Collect Willie and make your way home, round by the church.'

Then, soaked to the skin, I ran like a deer for the slope leading to the Manse. In the end, panting and almost done, but still undetected by the gamekeeper, I staggered into the kitchen and laid our catch at my mother's feet.

Archie was killed in the Second World War, on the plain of Gerbini in Sicily. Rona died in 1949, soon after winning the Gold Medal at the Gaelic Mod. But Willie, now senior skipper with the Anchor Line, he and I still remember that triumphant evening and the grace my father said as he lifted the cover off the steaming fish: *'Lord, we ask Thy blessing upon these mercies. Accept of our thanks and forgive us our sins.'*

We remember, too, that the Moderator nearly forgot to close his eyes.

My father, the Rev. Angus John MacVicar, MA, JP, was a chaplain in the First World War, for a time in Salonika. Afterwards we called him the Padre. He brought us up with old-fashioned strictness and left it to my mother, who was no slouch as a disciplinarian herself, to soften with a smile and words of comfort the abrasive impact of his rule. This impact was often physical as well as spiritual.

His standards of conduct were high. We found it hard to live up to them and were often inclined to resent being judged and condemned without trial.

Mingling with our thoughts in this direction was something else that worried us. Why was everything about our Presbyterian form of worship so stern and black? On the one hand we sang hymns which told us to 'let all with heart and voice before His throne rejoice'. On the other hand people came to church and sat in their pews with sombre clothes and grave faces as if they considered joy a mortal sin.

We knew, of course, that it all had something to do with mourning for the death of Christ. But if Christ died to make us happy, as people kept telling us, why was everybody so gloomy about it? Apart from everything else, it didn't seem fair to Him. We wanted to ask the Padre about this but weren't sure he'd understand: he might suddenly assume the aspect of Doré's *Avenging Angel,* as reproduced in the big family Bible, and accuse us of something terrible, like blasphemy.

At the time we were unaware that behind every dog-collar a human being is struggling to get out. The truth never dawned on us until the day the Padre had a puncture in his bicycle and decided to sort it himself.

I must explain that, besides being 'short in the grain', the Padre has always been singularly helpless as far as anything mechanical is concerned. That lovely summer morning, as

I saw a stranger yestreen:
I put food in the eating place,
Drink in the drinking place,
Music in the listening place:
And in the sacred name of the Triune,
He blessed myself and my house, my cattle and my dear
    ones.
And the lark said in her song,
'Often, often, often comes the Christ in the stranger's
    guise.'

The Padre's native language was the Gaelic, which
accounts for his habit of saying 'sugar-loaf' for 'loaf-sugar'
and 'warming-house party' for 'house-warming party', as he
mentally translates from the Gaelic idiom. He often tells
people about this. 'The boys,' he says—and by 'boys' he
means Willie and Kenneth and John and me, who can
muster over two hundred years between us—'the boys,' he
says, 'are always teasing me about it—how I'm inclined to
put the horse before the cart!'

Even at the age of 92, the Padre still puts first things first.

The Padre's good points were often camouflaged by an
irascible manner. The same can be said about Maimie. It
was a cross my mother had to bear, but she bore it with
remarkable fortitude.

Soon after his ordination and induction to the parish of
Duror, Argyll, in 1907—this was three years before he came
to Southend—the Padre married Marsali (Marjorie) Mac-
Kenzie, the youngest daughter of an Appin farmer. He was
lucky. Cheerfully, for the next fifty-six years, she lived
with his bouts of lethargy and energy, of bad temper and
charm. Gladly she bore him five sons and a daughter and,
with Maimie's help, did all the work, domestic and paro-
chial, which left him free for what he considered more
important duties. She scarcely ever had a holiday: seldom
was there any money to spare for that. In any case, her burn-

ing ambition was constantly for her husband and children. If they were happy, she was happy, too.

She loved parties and plenty of people about the house. When we were growing up in Southend, the Manse on a winter's night was often full of youngsters, singing, playing the piano, ruining the frail Edwardian drawing-room furniture with rough versions of 'Musical Chairs' and 'Fire, Air and Water'. On summer evenings the huge and shaggy front lawn, surrounded by aged trees, was an open playground for any children in the parish who cared to come. They came in droves, and we cut our hands and feet and tore our clothes scrambling on walls and roof-tops at games of 'Smuggle the Keg' and 'Kick the Can'.

In her younger days my mother herself took part in some of our games, with vigour and spirit. For forty years she had a bad knee, the result of a fall while trying to beat us at 'hop, step and jump' on gravel in front of the Manse. I always play hard to win, as a writer, as a golfer, as an amateur dramatist at competitive Festivals. But defeat doesn't worry me because it happens often and it usually makes somebody else extremely happy. I learned this way of looking at things from my mother.

With the parishioners in general and with the members of the Woman's Guild in particular she was popular. Her tact, unlike the Padre's, was unvarying, even in the most trying circumstances. The Padre can never hide his personal likes and dislikes. She could, though we knew that underneath it all her own loves and dislikes were more permanent than his.

She fluttered her big, dark green eyes at elders in the Kirk Session and they promptly voted her new paint and wallpaper for the sitting-room. She went to the houses visited by death or by the shame of an illegitimate child and there wept with the women and shared their grief. The women recovered. So did she. But after each of those occasions, we noticed, she became a little older, her gaiety a little more an act of will.

Her will was stronger than the Padre's: her faith, too,

perhaps. When unhappiness or tragedy occurred within the family it was she who disciplined her feelings and tried to persuade the rest of us that good can come out of evil. It was she who continually cajoled us into trying to 'make good' in a worldly sense, encouraging us to try again when we failed our school and university exams and the Padre threatened to deport us to the salt mines. I like to think that none of us let her down too badly. For myself, when sin lurks at the back of my mind, the thought of her anxious but always affectionate eyes is often enough to defeat it.

She was a staunch Tory all her life. When the Padre and I voted Liberal or Labour, as the fancy took us, she was deeply disappointed, not because we opposed her, but because she grieved for our immortal souls.

She and I were alone together when I was born in Duror in October 1908. We were alone together when she died in Southend in October 1963. Her last thought was for the Padre, how he was going to manage without her.

At her funeral, which took place on my birthday, we were all conscious that a strong anchor-chain had been broken.

When our parents came to Southend at the Mull of Kintyre, where five of us were born, they brought Maimie with them, a young girl whose actual name was Jessie MacLaren and whose home was in Perthshire. That was in 1910. Forty-seven years later, when they retired to the old United Free Church Manse in Southend, Maimie was still there, five feet nothing of flashing temper and implacable discipline.

We were always careful how we treated her. When she was in good humour we could pull her leg as much as we liked; but if somebody—or something—had upset her we walked gingerly, like explorers on the edge of a volcano.

She was one of the few people of whom the Padre was inclined to be afraid. None of us will ever forget the morning when she went into the larder for a bone for the soup. Passing through, on his way out to the garden, and seeing the larder door open, he absent-mindedly closed it and put the catch on. There being no handle on the inside, Maimie suddenly became a prisoner, stuck in the dark among chicken carcases and cold potatoes and jars of beetroot, until half-an-hour later my mother came downstairs to the kitchen and heard her shouting and banging on the door with the bone.

The Padre was summoned in from the garden to apologise, which he did in a pseudo-humble way. If he'd left it at that everything might have been all right. But he had—and still has—a kind of genius for putting his foot in it. He started to giggle, perhaps with a touch of nervous hysteria. 'One thing, Maimie,' he said, 'you wouldn't have starved in there!'

Maimie was not amused.

The day wore on. We sat around the big dining-room table and she brought in the soup: she would go on doing her duty even if it killed her. She put the tureen in front of my mother, stood back a little and said: 'If some people would concentrate on writing their sermons and stay out of the kitchen, we'd all get on a great deal better!' Then she stalked out, in a brittle silence.

Looking back on it now, I don't know how she put up with us all. But in sickness and in health, in joy and in sorrow, there she was, rushing about, scolding, exhorting, swearing to herself in the Gaelic. We all experienced the rough edge of her tongue—all except my mother, who had a way with her—but if anybody in the parish said anything about us in Maimie's hearing, then there was trouble. The Padre was not alone in being scared of her.

She seldom took a day off. In the matter of longer holidays she was like our parents: she always insisted she didn't want them, which sounds unlikely to me. Once she did leave us, when her mother was ill. At the end of six months she came back, sharp as ever, demanding to see what kind of a mess the kitchen was in.

We used to wonder why she never married: though tiny she had been good-looking in her day. As always straightforwardly curious, Archie once asked her about this, and the answer he got was quick and to the point. '*Chiall beannachd mi*, how on earth could I have got married, with all you lot to look after!' But she had a photo in her trunk, the photo of a young man in a First World War uniform. She said he was her cousin, who had been killed. But she said it in a quiet way—and she wasn't usually so quiet—and I still wonder about that photograph.

She was an actress in her way, and won many prizes for reciting poetry at the local Gaelic Mod. As a rule, of course, the Padre was one of the judges, so her success, though in general thoroughly deserved, wasn't altogether surprising.

She had a big repertoire, too, of recitations in English.

Our favourite was *Barbara Freitchie,* a forgotten epic of the American War of Independence. '*And up spake Barbara Freitchie then, bowed with her four score years and ten. "Shoot if you must this old grey head, but spare my country's flag," she said.*' By this time Willie was usually sobbing on her lap, while Archie and I, on cushions by her feet, struggled with unmanly tears.

Her own favourite was a poem about Flora MacCambridge, a young Southend nurse who in 1647 rescued her year-old charge, James Ranald MacDonald, from the Massacre of Dunaverty. 'Now, boys,' Maimie used to say when she had finished, 'let Flora be an example to you. She was afraid and she was lonely, but she did her duty. Remember the words of the poem: "Faithful and just was Flora, so her reward is sure." '

When she died in 1961 she willed all her savings to the four of us who were left. We each got £40.

The month of May always reminds me of our childhood in the Manse.

Everything was fresh and green and vivid. The salmon were plentiful in the burn and the peewits, not yet poisoned and decimated by agricultural insecticides, wheeled and called on the high moors. We made rafts out of planks of

wood and old petrol tins and tried to drown each other in
the burn. We climbed trees and burrowed in bramble
bushes looking for birds' eggs. Young ruffians we were,
cruel, thoughtless, snatching a wren's egg from her secret
nest and shaking with excitement as we made a hole in each
end with a pin and blew it dry.

I think all the innocent and the young have a cruel streak.
As we grow up we may learn to appreciate the values of
kindness, of beauty and of self-discipline; but the only way
the young can learn is from the example of older folk.

We were fortunate that the older folk in our case were
our parents—and Maimie. If we failed to live up to their
high ethical standards, as we all did at various times and
places, the fault was not theirs.

2

Hebridean Heritage

OUR ancestors went to North Uist from Argyll some six hundred years ago, as clerics, teachers of young men for the priesthood. Hence the name MacVicar, son of the Vicar.

Hence, also, I suspect, a family tendency to start preaching on any subject at the drop of a hat. How the ancestral MacVicars in *Tir Nan Og*, the Land of the Ever Young, must envy me my chance of publishing books and of talking on radio and television.

In the late sixteenth century the greater part of North Uist was owned and administered by a Donald MacVicar and his four sons. For a long time, however, the MacDonalds of Sleat in Skye had been directing envious eyes on the Mac-Vicar holdings. At last, when Donald was away on political business in Edinburgh, Hugh MacDonald, 'son of Archibald the Clerk', crossed from Skye with a strong bodyguard. Under an oath of friendship he invited the four brothers to a conference on *Dun an Sticir,* an island fort in one of the numerous lochs. That night, as they feasted, MacDonald's men drew their dirks and killed the brothers. When Donald MacVicar returned home he found his four sons dead and the MacDonalds in possession of North Uist. Like Mac-Gregor of the song, he was left 'sonless and landless'.

Afterwards the MacVicars became mere tenants and were eventually integrated with the crofting communities of the island.

The four MacVicars who died by treachery had three sisters. One of them composed a lament for her brothers, and a copy of *Oran Chlann a Phiocair,* 'The Song of the

Clan MacVicar', is in my father's possession. In the original
Gaelic it is a cry of agony and vengeance wrung from a
woman's heart. A modern translation into English has been
made by Professor D. S. Thomson of Glasgow University.
Here are three out of more than a dozen verses:

> Tall man from the Coolin hills,
> Light is your step, strong your blow.
> My seven curses on your foster mother
> That she did not press you with knee and elbow
> Before you killed the brothers.

> The Vicar came from the Lowlands
> And did not find one of the brothers alive.
> He found Marion and he found Mary,
> And he found me, wretch that I am,
> Not among the number of the dead.

> Hugh, son of Archibald the Clerk,
> When you lie down, do not rise whole:
> May your entrails be in the tail of your garment.
> May the news of your death come to the women of Sleat,
> And may I have a share in it.

When the Padre was a boy the standard of life in North Uist
was no better than in tribal Africa today. The savage conditions must appear almost incredible to anyone under the
age of fifty.

The 'black' house thatched with heather in which he was
born was like a smoke-filled hut in the wilds of Madagascar.
It had two rooms, a kitchen and a bedroom, with two doors
at opposite sides of the building. The windows were mere
slits in the stone walls. A fire of peat smouldered day and
night in the middle of the earthen floor in the kitchen, and a
hole in the roof let the smoke out. The beds were of straw,
which was changed twice a year in June and November. The
only light on dark evenings was a *cruiskan,* a small dish of
oil with a wick in it.

There were no amenities of any kind. My father's wash-basin was a pail, his toilet the open *machair*. His drinking water was drawn from a common well.

His father was a crofter, Angus MacVicar of Claddach, Kirkibost, who lived like his neighbours at subsistence level. The only money which ever came his way was when he had a cow or a sheep to sell; and out of that he had to pay the rent and other bills. His two children, Mary and Angus John (the Padre), went barefoot from April to October.

Indian meal porridge was the staple diet. Fruit and vegetables were almost unknown. A little kale might be grown for winter broth, and at Christmas and New Year a loaf of bread and a few apples might be bought as a treat for the young ones. 'We liked the bread best,' the Padre says, 'especially when jam was available.'

Between the 'black' houses of North Uist and the brave new villages of Scotland today, what a difference in ninety years. What a difference, too, between a philosophy based on the survival of the fittest and one concerned with the upholding of human dignity and well-being. Some politicians declare that they see no sign of the country getting better, that the people were healthier and happier in 'the good old days'. In the Padre's opinion this kind of talk is a load of old rubbish—and he should know. (Sometimes, when he tries even harder to be 'with it', he calls it a 'load of wallop-cods'. We know what he means.)

But his memories of a forgotten breed of island folk— the men and women of North Uist who were old when he was a boy—are warmer and more precious to him than those concerned with material disadvantages.

He speaks with affectionate pride of his grandfather, yet another Angus MacVicar, who was something of a 'character'.

In his youth he had a reputation for strength and agility. Unaided, he could lift a plough into a cart, and he was champion barrel-jumper of North Uist. As far as I can discover, barrel-jumping is a sport no longer practised. A dozen or more empty herring-barrels were placed side by side in a row, and the idea was to find the man who, without pause, could jump in and out of the greatest number of barrels. My great-grandfather's record, I believe, was fourteen.

He seems also, in his bachelor days, to have had an eye for the girls. The Padre glosses over this aspect of the story but, when pressed, admits that we may have more blood relations in the Hebrides than we imagine.

More than once, as he grew older, my great-grandfather and his cousin sailed in an open boat from North Uist to Glasgow with a cargo of eggs and other native produce and returned to the island laden with groceries and sheaves of black willows for the making of lobster-creels. In those days, at the beginning of last century, such a journey must have appeared to less adventurous spirits as difficult and dangerous as a Chichester journey today.

As well as being a crofter, Old Angus did a sideline as a dealer and was the first in North Uist to buy eggs at three-pence a dozen.

Among his other activities, he was a regular churchgoer. He told my father that it was usual for himself and his contemporaries to engage in all kinds of sport—leaping and running and putting the stone—not to mention barrel-jumping—before the services began. 'And what was wrong with that?' says the Padre, when he assumes his occasional role as a benign liberal philosopher. But the mind boggles at what might have happened had his sons tried to put this excellent idea into practice.

Old Angus was a strong man, both physically and morally. When the Disruption took place in 1843 he was an elder of the Church of Scotland, and though many of his friends joined the new Free Church he refused to desert the leaking ship. He recognised that at the time of the Clearances Church of Scotland ministers, with only a few gallant exceptions, had taken the side of the lairds: he condemned them as bitterly as did his neighbours. But his argument was, 'My

Church, right or wrong'; and in any case, he never believed that ministers made or marred the Church.

Like his grandson, the Padre, he was never a man to submit meekly to an opponent. Once, at a funeral, he was upholding the Old Kirk against a number of Free Churchmen. Unctuously, one of them said to him: 'You have chosen the broad way, Angus, but do not let us quarrel about it. We are told in the Scriptures that the wheat and the tares are allowed to grow together in the same field until the harvest.' My great-grandfather nearly blew a gasket. 'Are you calling me a tare?' he demanded, as a prelude to violent action. This became a saying in North Uist, and I have heard it quoted by many people in the Islands.

The Padre describes him as steeped in the Columban tradition that we should be just and merciful, kind to the needy and hospitable to a stranger, though I suspect his beliefs were sorely tested if the stranger turned out to belong to the Free Church. When he was an old man, and blind, the Padre remembers him saying to his daughter before the frugal evening meal: 'Ishbel, have you set the stranger's place?'

The Padre goes on: 'He chose a place for private prayer between two slabs of rock on the shore. On Sunday evenings and at times of sorrow he would kneel there, facing the east with clasped hands, making his requests known to God and seeking forgiveness, mercy and help. In my memory's eye I can still see him returning to the house from his place of prayer, bent and blind, wearing a Highland bonnet and with a staff in his hand.'

Until he was six years old the Padre could speak no English. Then he went to the parish school at Paible, where he learnt his second language and made acquaintance with the three Rs. In this he was more fortunate than his father and mother, whose education was derived solely from the Church schools, where they were taught to read the Bible and the Shorter Catechism, in Gaelic.

In this primitive environment, with its cultural and
material poverty, the old people of North Uist, against all
the odds, retained their faith. In some respects, however, it
was a sad and submissive faith, a kind of fatalism which
probably stemmed from the Evictions and the Clearances,
when men, women and children were herded aside to make
way for sheep and when it seemed that nobody cared,
neither lairds nor ministers nor Government officials.

I think a saving grace was their sense of humour. They
loved a ceilidh on a winter's night, exchanging yarns about
characters they knew; and though the smoke curling up to
the hole in the roof made them cough, they would be quick
to laugh as well.

It seems that a favourite butt for those ceilidh yarns was
a second-cousin of the Padre's. He was so highly superstitious
and afraid of the dark that when he and his wife went to
bed, with the wind moaning through the thatch, he would
plead with her: 'Morag, don't you go to sleep before I do!'

The captains of the mail steamers which called at Lochmaddy in North Uist also provided stories worth retelling.

There was one old character who always pronounced 'th'
as 's', a common habit among Gaelic speakers. Once, in the
Kyles of Lochalsh, he was hailed by the anxious owner of a
small yacht, who shouted up to him: 'I'm sinking, skipper!
I'm sinking!' To which the skipper, leaning comfortably on
the bridge, replied: 'Well, well, and what are you sinking
about?'

Another tale concerns a North Uist girl travelling by
steamer to Glasgow, where she hoped to enter domestic service. Half way across the Minch she was asked to show her
ticket. As she fumbled for it in her handbag, a testimonial
to her character supplied by her local minister was snatched
away by the wind. She began to cry, believing she might miss
the chance of getting work if she were unable to produce a
reference. But the skipper was equal to the occasion. 'Never
you mind, lassie,' he said. 'I'll give you a certificate that will
see you through.' And there and then he sat down and wrote

it: 'This is to certify that on the night of the seventh November in the Minch, on board the s.s. *Sheila,* Kirsty MacLean lost her character.'

But the ceilidh yarns were not all humorous. A different side of the Hebridean nature can be found in a story the Padre often tells, in a voice suitably hushed and solemn.

On the night of the Tay Bridge disaster in December 1879, my grandfather and grand-uncle in North Uist made fast their stacks of corn and peat. Then they went into the house and read the Bible together and offered a prayer: a prayer especially for those in danger at sea. A week or so later, the skipper of a steamer berthed at Lochmaddy saw my grand-uncle on the pier. He called him on board and told him that on the night of the great gale he had been at sea and in great mental and physical distress. Then, suddenly, as he stood on the heaving bridge, he had seen my grand-uncle's face before him in the storm-filled dark and peace had come to him.

I wish I could believe in the efficacy of prayer as unconditionally as my forebears did.

The first time the Padre possessed an overcoat was when he left North Uist at the age of sixteen to go to a secondary school at Kingussie on the mainland of Inverness-shire. He had just won a bursary of £15 a year.

At the end of last century, when the State was only beginning to take an interest in ordinary individuals—except when it wanted them for the Army or Navy—this money was administered by the Church, which, through the dark ages, was the only source of education for those whom we now call the underprivileged.

The Padre lived in lodgings in Kingussie, sharing a room with a fellow pupil for which they both paid half-a-crown a week. They bought their own food. The house had no toilet, and water came from a pump in the street.

He was fond of sport, however, especially shinty, and he grew like a young deer in his new environment.

On his eighteenth birthday he decided he must start shaving and was faced with the problem of purchasing the necessary equipment. 'In my innocence and ignorance,' he says, 'I thought the shops in Kingussie were similar to those in North Uist which sold everything from a needle to an anchor, so one evening I entered the first shop I came to in the High Street and asked for a razor, soap and a brush. But this in fact was a draper's shop, and I can still see the girls at the counter laughing and giggling as they said they didn't stock such things. I felt very humiliated.'

When he went to Glasgow University, he found that the students there had no Shinty Club. With the help of a few friends, therefore, at a meeting held in a pub at the corner of Park Road and Gibson Street, he founded one and was appointed its first Captain, in 1901. The Club was immediately successful and has been ever since, living up to its Ossianic motto: 'It is they who would play the shinty, as fleet as the roe bucks on the rough mountainside.'

The University has a framed photo of that first shinty team, with the captain in the front row sporting a Kitchener of Khartoum moustache. He looks a tough guy, and it seems he was just that, always ready to fly off the handle if foiled by an opponent. But even St Columba found it hard to maintain a Christian attitude when somebody struck him on the ankle with a shinty-stick.

The Padre was also a football fan. He remembers how disappointed he felt one Saturday in 1902 when Scotland was playing England at Ibrox Park and he had to miss the match because of a History examination. But late that afternoon, as he walked down from the University to his lodgings, he wondered if perhaps the exam had been a blessing in disguise, because there, in Kelvingrove Street, he was confronted by a blaring poster: DISASTER AT IBROX. A temporary wooden stand had collapsed. Many spectators had been killed and hundreds injured.

In 1906 he passed his final Divinity exams with commendation. Indeed, he informs his not so fortunate sons that he passed every University exam he ever sat. We are not so sure. Old men can forget.

That same year, in May, he was licensed by his home Presbytery in Carinish Church in North Uist. His grandfather had been an elder there. His parents worshipped there each Sunday. The Church is situated only a short distance away from the ruins of Trinity Temple, where our ancestors of long ago taught and trained young men for the priesthood.

Near Trinity Temple, on the south side, stands a grass-grown chapel known as the Temple of the MacVicars. Tradition has it that twelve of the name are buried inside its tumbled walls, including those who came to the island from Argyll. It is not so strange, therefore, that the Padre became a minister and that we all have the urge to preach on a variety of subjects, sacred and secular. It is not so strange, either, that he has always felt at home in Argyll, especially in his adopted parish of Southend, where St Columba first stepped ashore in Scotland more than fourteen hundred years ago.

For the Padre the transition from the open air communions of his Hebridean boyhood to the annual Columban Conventicle in Southend was also natural enough. Like Columba, his forebears preached a religion bound up with ordinary things: a religion which allowed love and reverence for all men to sweeten the action not only of Sunday but of every day. He preached the same practical doctrine, flavoured by the salt tang of the sea, with a hint behind it of the fairy land of *Tir Nan Og* over the horizon.

There is another reason why he liked Southend so well that for over forty-seven years he ministered to its people and for another twelve lived there in retirement.

He was a crofter's son. He loved the *machair* and the sea and as a student on holiday had taken his share of working on the land. From the beginning he felt at home among the fields of Southend, with the fresh wind blowing over them from the Firth of Clyde. He could also discuss with some expertise the problems of the farmers and farm-workers who made up most of Southend's population of approximately five hundred.

During his long ministry he always kept a close eye on agricultural progress. Modern farming bears no relation to the scythe and sickle methods of his Hebridean youth. 'If my father and grandfather saw a combine harvester,' he says, 'they wouldn't know what to make of it. The big herds of cows, the milking machines and the milk tankers would be another eye-opener for them. They'd be surprised, too, by the wages and conditions of farm-workers at the present time. I remember in North Uist, eighty years ago, a man was lucky if he got £3 in the half year, working day and daily from six in the morning until six at night.'

Of course, when he came to Southend at first, farming was a less remunerative occupation than it is today. I remember myself, in 1930, when agricultural boards, grants and subsidies were mere glints in a planner's eye, that farmers in Southend were forced to sell their milk at 3½d a gallon and that the top annual wage for a farm-worker was £60.

The Padre also discovered that conditions in most of the farm cottages in his new parish were not a great deal better than in North Uist. Eventually he decided to try to remedy this.

For some years he had been a co-opted member of Argyll Education Committee. Now, in 1929, he was proposed and seconded as a candidate to represent Southend on the County Council.

Then sensation: a sensation which caused my Tory mother to flush with embarrassment, Maimie to invent new Gaelic expletives and the family to shiver with excitement. The Duke of Argyll's factor was put up as a rival candidate, and we were painfully aware that at the time almost every farmer in the parish was a tenant of the Duke's.

Unhappily, as far as the family were concerned, only Willie, Rona and Kenneth were directly involved in the drama. At this stage Archie and I were at Glasgow University, while John, aged two, was more interested in his own affairs than in those of the Padre. Archie and I, however, were kept in close touch with developments by means of daily despatches from the battle-front.

The first thing that happened was that the Duke himself called on the Padre and suggested he should withdraw. But though the kilted MacCalein Mhor paid most of the tiends that went to make up his stipend, the Padre said 'No!' in a remarkably loud voice—Rona and Kenneth were listening, breathless, outside the drawing-room door—and the election was on.

A hot campaign was mounted against the idea of new houses, which was the principal buttress of the Padre's programme. 'What was good enough for their fathers is good enough for them!' 'If they're not in a tied cottage they'll demand more wages!' 'New houses for that lot? They'll put coals in the bath!'

An important parishioner published his views that subsidised council houses would 'undermine the moral fibre' of the workers. In our state of political ignorance we thought it peculiar that an individual who had inherited his wealth and never done a day's work in his life should hold such a curious opinion. What about his own moral fibre?

Always a fighter, the Padre did his share of canvassing; and, fortunately, his bicycle stood up to the strain. Willie and Kenneth did their bit by keeping it oiled and greased.

A vote for the landlord, or a vote for the minister? The horrible dilemma was discussed in many homes. Those farmers who were not tenants of the Duke openly supported the Padre. The others kept quiet, though some expressed the opinion that a minister had no right to poke his nose into what was a political issue. At one house, however, he was told: 'Don't you worry, minister. Some of the men may vote for the Duke, but their women-folk are not thirled to him.'

At last the day for voting came, and, as the *Campbeltown Courier* said, there were more false faces in Southend on that occasion than at Hallowe'en. It appears, too, from accounts given by Willie, Rona and Kenneth, that as the hours went by life in the Manse became exceedingly grim. My mother could eat nothing; Maimie scuttled and screeched like an angry hen; the Padre kept calling for milk, with baking soda in it. (This was his usual tipple before facing the tensions of the pulpit each Sunday. In emergencies, St Paul recommended a little wine for the stomach's sake. The Padre favoured milk and baking soda.)

In the evening the result of the election was declared. The vote was for the minister by a two to one majority, which has always seemed to me to reflect not only the Padre's courage but also the humanity and good sense of his parishioners. There was joy in the Manse. For the first time in weeks a kind of serenity prevailed.

In due course, at a meeting of the County Council, the Padre moved the adoption of a report by the Medical Officer of Health recommending new houses for farmworkers, and the first step was taken in the housing programme for Argyll. Today there are thirty-six Council houses in Southend, and I have yet to hear of a tenant who puts coals in his bath.

As well as being a County Councillor and a member of the Education Committee, the Padre was for a period Clerk to the Synod of Argyll. He was also Clerk to the Presbytery of Kintyre for fifty years, a record in the Church of Scotland. I am sorry to report, however, that his grotesque handwriting makes it doubtful if anybody will ever know exactly what took place in the Presbytery of Kintyre from 1913 to 1963.

Once he convened a Presbytery meeting 'in hunc affectum', and on the postcard his scrawl was rendered by the printers as 'in warm affection'. When the meeting assembled, the Rev. Kenneth MacLeod of Gigha, Gaelic poet and author of The Road to the Isles, rose to his feet waving the card. Brown eyes twinkling, but with a deadpan expression, he said: 'For once, dear brethren, may the Clerk's prayer be granted!'

The Padre's practical application of religion had two notable results. In 1952 he was responsible for the establishment of an Eventide Home in Campbeltown, though he himself would never dream of living in it, being too independent, too much thirled to the countryside. Then, after he had retired in 1957 and could, therefore, himself derive no benefit, he fathered an Overture from the Synod of Argyll, eventually approved by the General Assembly, whereby the stipends of ministers in remote Highland and Hebridean parishes were increased by £150.

The Padre amassed no material wealth; but he has always provided his family with plenty of excitement and, at times, amusement. He has always been involved in the life of his parish and of the Church as a whole, probing, arranging, arguing, often quarrelling violently with those who disagree with him.

The old clerics and preachers went from Argyll to North Uist. He came from North Uist to Argyll and has proved himself, I think, their worthy descendant.

3

The Face of My Parish

THE Padre, my mother and Maimie and I (then aged eighteen months) left Duror in 1910 and settled happily in the parish of Southend. With the exception of five years at Glasgow University and five years serving abroad during the last war, I have lived in Southend ever since.

I was lucky. I found a job which permitted me to stay. Rona, too, was able to return from University and teach in Campbeltown. But Archie and Willie, Kenneth and John—schoolmaster and ship's captain, minister and doctor—they all had to leave in order to follow their chosen professions. In each of them, however, there remained a warm sentiment for their native parish.

I had a choice. As a writer I might have made more money working from a city base. But it has always seemed to me that the advantages of living in the country, particularly in Southend, far outweigh the disadvantages.

It is true we are a hundred and fifty miles from Glasgow by road and more than five hundred miles from London. But British European Airways can convey us to Glasgow in an hour and to London in three hours. On one bad-tempered occasion, owing to traffic jams, it took a publisher friend of mine three hours to take me by car from his home in Chipstead to his Bloomsbury office.

The sea and the prevailing wind from the west make Southend's arable fields and high moorland fresh and clean. There are no problems of pollution, as long as one doesn't object —as I don't—to the powerful odour of cattle dung newly spread on stubble or to the stink of rotted silage being carted out to feed wintering stirks.

The climate is generally mild, which may be due to the influence of the Gulf Stream flowing past the shores of Ireland, only eleven miles away across the North Channel. Hard frost is rare, and a heavy snowfall occurs only about once in every ten years. We get plenty of rain, and the grass fields coloured emerald green are proof of it. Sometimes sou'-easters whip the sea into a white fury of spray, and on these occasions salt accumulates on the windows of houses by the shore and has to be cleaned off twice a day. Before the establishment of a coastguard station vessels ran aground on our rock-toothed coast at an alarming rate, and some of those ancient wrecks can still be seen at low water.

The scenery is thrilling. The Firth of Clyde fans out to the east, where Ailsa Craig, nicknamed Paddy's Milestone, stands sentinel. To the south and west the Mountains of Mourne are like silhouettes in a Walt Disney cartoon. To the north lie Islay's slate-grey hills and the improbable Paps of Jura.

Sixty years ago, when the Padre came to the parish, there was poverty in Southend. The farmers were little more than peasants. Their labourers lived either in damp, insanitary cothouses on the farms or in noisome hovels in the village. I remember a back-alley called 'Teapot Lane', where fish-heads, tea-leaves and human excreta were thrown out into a grated drain which ran past the front doors. Some families didn't even have a house: they lived in caves by the shore, like animals, and only occasionally was their lot alleviated by the distribution of Poor Law half-crowns by the Parish Council.

There was a high incidence of tuberculosis, illegitimacy and drunkenness. The tuberculosis came from the milk of ill-nourished cattle. Illegitimacy and drunkenness were by-products of a hard and comfortless existence and a human need to forget.

Today, thanks to forward-looking policies in respect of

agriculture and housing, thanks to grants, subsidies and the Welfare State, there is no poverty in Southend. There is no tuberculosis, either, and even before the introduction of 'the pill' and the breathalyser illegitimacy and drunkenness had become much less common.

Since the Duke of Argyll sold his Kintyre estates in 1955 most of the farmers own their farms. Their lands have been made rich by skilful, scientific husbandry—which started a long time ago with the introduction of the wild white clover —and nowadays they, too, have become passing rich. Most farming families possess two cars. Tractors have taken over from horses, powering such weird implements as rotavators, silorators, hay tedders, combine harvesters and dung spreaders. Huge creamery tanks prowl the side roads collecting milk, tuberculin-tested milk which has been drawn from the cows' udders by electrically motivated machines and conveyed by pipe-lines to hygienic storage-tanks. Sixty years ago cows were milked by hand. Some of the hands were grubby, and dirt and dung often spattered into the pail. Today, milk is never exposed to the air until it appears on our breakfast tables.

The condition of the farm workers has undergone a similar revolution. Most of them are now comfortably housed by the County Council. Some possess cars and motor-bikes. There is no distinction, as there used to be, between employers and employees at a dance, at the Sports Club or on the golf course.

But in these days of comparative affluence the farmers of Southend, like farmers elsewhere, may be facing another wind of change. The Common Market looms on the horizon. In a few years' time, according to the scientists, milk will be manufactured artificially and cows, finicky beasts at the best, with a long and troublesome history of foot-and-mouth disease, tuberculosis and brucellosis, will become redundant.

Quo vadis?

Meanwhile, however, though Rome may be burning in

the distance, in Southend we continue to whistle. A minister, a doctor, a schoolmaster and two schoolmistresses guide our spiritual and physical footsteps. We have two churches, one of them recently closed, two primary schools, two public halls for recreation, two hotels for relaxation, two caravan parks for visitors and two shops where, with average luck, we can buy anything from original paintings to contraceptives. One of the shops contains the Post Office.

We also have a maddeningly beautiful eighteen-hole golf course, standard scratch score 63, of which, I may say, I know every blade of grass; and it is my proud boast that through the years I have been both Champion and Captain of Dunaverty Golf Club. (S. L. McKinlay, editor of the *Glasgow Evening Times* and golf writer *par excellence*, declares that in high summer our greens are like boilerplates, but Sam is talking through a hole in his Walker Cup 'bunnet'.)

The main attraction of Southend, however, is that its five hundred inhabitants, ninety per cent of whom owe their livelihood to agriculture, constitute a real community. This may be due in part to its geographical location at the tip of the Mull of Kintyre, where it is bounded on three sides by the sea and on a fourth by high hills, through which only two roads lead out to Campbeltown. But there is another reason. Since everybody in the parish knows the final detail about his or her neighbour's character and affairs, we see no point in practising irksome gimmicks to attract attention, no point in 'keeping up appearances' with employers and influential acquaintances. The result is a magic of friendly hospitality, a spirit of one for all and all for one which is becoming increasingly rare, even in Scotland.

There is practical proof of this spirit in our thriving parish organisations: the Church, the Woman's Guild, the 'Rural', the Drama Club, the Sports Club, the Golf Club, the Badminton Club, the Darts Club, the Country Dancing. The trouble is, we haven't enough nights in the week to enjoy them all.

This is not to say, however, that we don't quarrel among ourselves. The imminent closing of one of the churches, the rights and wrongs of capital punishment, the proposed repair and restoration of a local hall, the desirability of using 'the pill', the planned erection of a new coastguard look-out on the historic summit of Dunaverty Rock, the agricultural problems relevant to the Common Market, the interpretation of a new rule on the golf course, the question of apartheid in Rhodesia, coupled with the name of Ian Smith—all of these are subjects for controversy, for loud declarations of policy and intent which appear to divide the parish and even to annihilate the peace of family life. Passions rise, and a few verbal blows may be struck in the public bar at the Inn. But in time the current argument is exhausted, another one flares up, individuals assume new attitudes and the enemies of yesterday become the friends of today.

Pakistanis, Negroes, Jews and mid-Europeans move among us with goods to sell and cars to hire. Perhaps we are lucky in that all the 'foreigners' we know are solid and respectable citizens; but the fact remains that I have never found the slightest trace of colour or racial prejudice anywhere in Southend.

There is very little political prejudice either. We have no clear-cut Right and Left. Mr Heath is not always opposed to Mr Wilson. Sometimes they combine against an alliance of Mr Crossman and Mr Maudling. In other words, it is a healthy, reasonably integrated community, and many of the summer visitors to the hotels, the farms and the caravan sites become part of it.

I think the greatest challenge facing us in the last quarter of the twentieth century is the need for community. In this era of fantastic technological advances in space and industry, of new medical discoveries, of the permissive—or amoral—society, of the gospel according to Wheatley, we are creating a life in which many people are beginning to feel helpless to influence events. Communities are essential to provide interests and pursuits in which an individual can join and not simply be an onlooker. Otherwise suspicion and distrust are bound to go on growing, not only between racial groups and between employers and employees but also between the old and the young, reactionary die-hards and revolutionary skinheads, schoolmasters and parents, police and the public. Only by being part of a community can we get to know each other really well. And only by knowing each other really well can we begin to understand —and perhaps even to love—our neighbours.

As I see it, a community depends to a great extent on two factors often liable to be overlooked: a high ethical standard in its family life and a tacit recognition by the old that youth must be given an important place on its decision-making bodies. By all means let us argue until the fur flies. Let us also, however, have a charitable respect for each other's personality and human dignity, so that when the arguments are over we can let our hair down and have a ball together.

A focal point in Southend is Dunaverty Rock. Now, as I write, I see it across the Bay, towering ninety feet above the water and the sand, a turf-coated lump of Old Red Sandstone which is also a hub of history.

As small boys in disgrace after committing a misdemeanour, my brothers and I often climbed it to let the keen wind on the top whip away our sorrow at the unfeeling attitudes of parents and teachers. I still climb it when I get out of tune with affairs, and the therapeutic qualities of height and grandeur and a salty breeze are still there.

The Rock is formed of pebbles from the shore of a primeval lake, pebbles gradually cemented together by sand and silt as the earth cooled. On its exposed surfaces are the fossil impressions of trilobites, small extinct shellfish which three hundred million years ago were the highest form of life.

The first men to see Dunaverty did so around 6000 B.C. They were Mesolithic men from Ireland with flint arrows

and flint tools stuck in their belts of reindeer hide, the first
human beings to settle in Kintyre after the Second Ice Age
and almost certainly the first inhabitants of Scotland:
Middle Stone Age men, small and slant-eyed, terrified of the
dark and the monsters of the dark.

They were followed by men of the Neolithic Age, then by
men of the Bronze Age and the Iron Age, whose arrow-
heads, drinking utensils and primitive tools have all been
dug up near the Rock. In place of terror those later inhabitants were beginning to recognise an ideal of trust, even of
love. Not far from Dunaverty there can be seen a stone
'barrow', its apex pointing to the east, where the sun-god
rose each morning. From this prehistoric grave archaeologists recently unearthed some tiny coloured beads, the
remains of a bracelet placed there on the grave of a child.

Today the golf course winds past Dunaverty Rock. Two
old life-boat sheds stand near it, both used by Archie
Cameron, the fisherman, as stores for nets and creels. On
the yellow beach that makes a half-mile curve between it and
my bungalow children erect sandcastles, while their parents
frolic in the sea or lie comfortably in the shade of the bent.
All peaceful in the summer sun.

But the history of Dunaverty, as we first discovered while
listening to Maimie's poem about Flora MacCambridge,
was anything but peaceful.

It once boasted a MacDonald castle, the fighting part on
the Rock itself, the living quarters for families and camp-
followers on the high dune which now separates it from the
golf course. Some of the crumbling ruins can still be seen
above the turf. Four hundred years ago this castle must have
seemed impregnable both from land and sea, a sullen place,
offering no point of weakness to an invader.

In May, 1647, the Marquis of Argyll came marching into
Kintyre with three thousand Campbells, part of Cromwell's
ironclad army. Near Tarbert the Royalist MacDonalds,
always bitter enemies of the Campbells, made an effort to
stop this bold advance; but their cavalry floundered to

disaster in a peat-bog at Rhunahaorine, and they fell back on their last stronghold, Dunaverty.

In command of the garrison was Lord Archibald Mac-Donald, whose wife had died a few months before, leaving him with a baby son, James Ranald. James Ranald's nurse was an eighteen-year-old Southend girl called Flora Mac-Cambridge.

For six weeks the Campbells besieged the Castle; but in a hot, dry June the water in the only well ran dry—occasionally it still runs dry in summer—and in the end it was thirst that defeated the MacDonalds. Lord Archibald surrendered to 'the mercy of Argyll', and, as might have been expected, the mercy of Argyll was death. 'Death', as that assiduous war correspondent Sir James Turner puts it, 'to every mother's son of the garrison'.

Two centuries later the bones of the dead were gathered by descendants of the clan and buried in a communal grave. A bleak, rectangular monument, it stands on the bare shoulder of an arable field near the Rock. The field is known as *machair a caistel,* 'the field of the castle'.

On the night before the massacre, however, Flora Mac-Cambridge made a plan to save James Ranald, heir to the ancient line. Round him she wrapped a plaid of Campbell tartan. Then, carrying him in her arms, she crept down from the Rock and began to run across the beach, away from Dunaverty, away from death.

But soon, while still stumbling barefoot over the wet, ribbed sand, she was stopped by a Campbell sentry. Her heart thumped in her throat.

'I am the wife of a Campbell soldier,' she said. 'See, my son wears the tartan.'

The sentry lifted a corner of the plaid. 'Strange!' he said. 'A Campbell mother whose baby has the MacDonald eyes! But go your way, girl. We have no quarrel with women and children.'

So Flora went to a cave under the cliff at Kiel, and there, feeding him on sheep's tallow and ewes' milk, she hid and looked after James Ranald until the Campbells had gone.

James Ranald grew up and eventually, by patient negotiation, brought about a lasting peace between the MacDonalds and the Campbells. He lies buried in the churchyard at Kiel, Southend, just over the wall from the big cave in which he and Flora had found refuge.

One day, about twenty years ago, a Mrs MacDonald from Rhodesia came to Southend to see the grave of her husband's ancestor. The Padre took her to the churchyard, showed her the tombstone and then, as he has so often done for the benefit of visitors, told the story of Flora MacCambridge. As a sequel he mentioned that James Ranald had married a daughter of the Stewarts of Bute.

The lady held out her left hand. 'I know,' she said. 'This is the ring he gave her.'

In Southend the Padre found heroic tales of clan warfare to gladden his romantic heart. He also found something else with which he had been familiar in North Uist. This was the spirit of Columba, the first saint of the Celtic Church, and at once it made him feel at home in his new parish.

There is a tradition, firmly supported by the historian Lucy Menzies, that before Columba settled in Iona in A.D. 563 he first landed at Southend: at Kiel, where the churchyard is, almost under the shadow of Dunaverty.

Let me say in passing, how firmly I believe in tradition. Take the walls of Jericho, for example. So-called scholars scoffed at the story of the trumpets blowing and the walls falling outwards. But when archaeologists dug down to the ancient city they found that the clay-brick walls *had* fallen outwards, and modern science confirmed that under the shrill blast of scores of trumpets this is exactly what *would* happen.

There is no need, however, to go digging for proof that Columba made his first landfall at the Mull of Kintyre. Knowledgeable seamen point out that fourteen hundred years ago anybody heading for Scotland from Derry, especially in a small boat made of wicker and hides, would never have attempted to sail north, directly to Iona, exposed all the way to the Atlantic winds and to the deadly tides which ring the Southern Hebrides. An expert sailor—and Columba was just that—would have made straight for the nearest land, which was the Mull of Kintyre.

On and around a green hillock above the churchyard at Kiel more proof can be found.

First, there is a flat rock in which are carved the prints of two right feet, known locally as St Columba's Footsteps. It is probable that the prints were there long before Columba's time, for use by newly elected chiefs when swearing an oath of fealty to their tribe. But I believe Columba also used the Footsteps, first facing the east and the rising sun, then turning north to address the people gathered on a steep hillside, a hillside which to this day is known in Gaelic as 'the shoulder of the congregation'.

Second, right beside the Footsteps, the remains of an ancient cell are outlined beneath the turf, a small crude church which may have been built by those who followed Columba.

Third, a few yards away from the hillock, behind the churchyard, there is a well whose water is supposed to have magic properties. Half the present population of Southend were baptised with it. The well is called St Columba's Well, and in the rock above is incised a cross on which the lichen never grows. Indeed, this is no wonder, because everybody who comes to see the well instinctively traces out the cross with a finger, and so the lichen is constantly rubbed away.

And fourth, what is even more interesting and more significant, less than a hundred yards from the Footsteps can be found a cave with a Druid altar inside. Still visible on the altar are the cup marks and the small channels which drained off the blood of the sacrifices.

Why is it that a close study of Columba's magic always reveals in the background an even older magic, represented in this case by the Footsteps, the well and the Druid altar?

The answer, I think, is that like Christian missionaries among the tribes of Africa today, Columba played it cool. He set up a little church beside a pagan temple and carved his cross above a pagan well and slowly and with courage came to terms with the Druid witch-doctors, building a new faith on the foundation of the old.

An old lady in North Uist once asked me, in the Gaelic: 'Are you going to the stones?' I failed to understand at first, but it was her way of saying, after all those centuries, 'Are you going to church?'

Today adventurous children clamber on Dunaverty Rock, searching among its crevices for bullets fired in the great siege. Under its ancient eye red farm tractors chug busily through the lazy ranks of holiday-makers. My friends and I play golf on the links adjoining it, forgetting in the heat of the moment that a missed putt is an unnoticed wrinkle in the graph of time. Fishermen whip the peat-brown Con, hopeful that a few salmon may have dodged upstream past Archie Cameron's nets at the mouth of the burn. The church bell rings on Sunday—the old bell with a crack in it that was salvaged from a wreck. The meetings of the Woman's Guild and the W.R.I. take place in un-changing succession. Ignoring the alien cultures of Brecht and Becket, we present plays by James Bridie, Joe Corrie and Jimmy Scotland, happy to make crowded audiences roll in the aisles and to win prizes at Community Drama Festivals, but always modest about our artistic importance. At the inn long-haired hippy-clad farmers' boys play darts and drink vodka and orange with their girls, while in the Dunaverty Hall descendants of Flora MacCambridge—my wife among them—play badminton, attend political meet-ings and dance to the latest pop music.

We all tend to ignore a future when the Rock will again become a mess of pebbles and slime, as it was in the beginning.

4

Magical Mystery Tour

ALL his life, in Southend, the Padre has been aware of the magic of Columba. So have I. But it is like a rainbow arch above Dunaverty, there one minute, gone the next.

A conscious search for it on my part means reading books about Columba, beginning with Adamnan, because in these books are marshalled the generally accepted facts about his early life in Ireland. They provide a necessary background to the Scottish stories and legends.

He was born in A.D. 521 near Gartan Lough in Donegal, the son of Felim, a chief of the royal tribe of O'Neill, and his wife, Eithne. (In parenthesis I note that the former Prime Minister of Northern Ireland, Captain Terence O'Neill, is a descendant of the same family.)

His birthday was a Thursday, 'when the tide began to flow', and I remember that old folk in the Hebrides can still recite this poem in the Gaelic:

> Day of Columba benign:
> Day to put the web in the warp,
> To put coracle on the brine:
> Day to hunt the heights,
> Day to put horses in harness
> And send herds to pasture.

I remember, too, how many young couples arrange to be married on a Thursday, because in Scotland it's supposed to be a lucky day for weddings.

His parents christened him Columba, the dove, and

trained him for the Church. But as he grew up, sturdy and strong, with an imperious temper which often got him into fights, the boys of the tribe had another name for him— Crimthann, the wolf.

When he was thirteen he entered a monastery school at Doire-Eithne in the green valley of the Leanan. Afterwards he studied at the Colleges of Moville and Clonard, the Oxford and Cambridge of ancient Ireland, and I am surprised to discover that each of those colleges had about three thousand students, including a number of women, and that the professors and lecturers were all learned men who had travelled widely in Europe, some as Christian missionaries.

He left Clonard an ordained priest; but he had also learned how to construct a boat, how to build a hut with branches and clay, how to plough and sow and cut the ripened corn. He had also acquired a taste for music and an urge to write poetry. And a phrase dropped by Adamnan makes me suspect that as a shinty player he was inclined to lose his temper with over-enthusiastic opponents. Sympathetically I reflect that it's not always easy to be a Christian when somebody hacks you on the ankle with a shinty-stick.

As the years passed, he founded many monasteries in Ireland whose names are like a poem: Derry and Drumhone, Durrow and Raphoe, Sords and Kells. But all the time the dove struggled with the wolf, and the continuous sparking between the two points supplied the power for a dynamic personality.

In his forty-second year it also changed the whole course of his life.

Finnian, his former professor at Moville, returned from a visit to Rome with a precious manuscript, a new translation of the Gospels by St Jerome. As a rule, Finnian jealously kept his books to himself, but he respected Columba's scholarship and allowed him to see this one. It proved so interesting that Columba made a copy for himself, in secret.

But Finnian found out, and the two men angrily went to law about it.

They appeared in court at Tara-of-the-Kings in Leinster, where Diarmit, High King of Ireland, delivered judgment; and I am astonished to learn that this judgment is the basis of our modern law of copyright: 'To every cow her calf, to every book its transcript. Therefore the copy made by you, Columba, belongs to Finnian.'

Columba was furious. He forgot his quarrel with Finnian and aimed his anger at the King. 'It is a wrong judgment!' he thundered. 'In battle will I be avenged!'

Diarmit began the Battle of Culdreimnhe in 562 by marching his men sunwise around a cairn, in accordance with Druidical rites. Columba blessed his followers and prayed to God for victory, though, as I study his reported words, I have a feeling that his conscience was troubling him and that he realised he might receive a dusty answer.

But at first his cause appeared to prosper. Diarmit was routed, and Columba's power became greater than ever, even though that power was more temporal than spiritual.

Then the tide turned. The clerics of Ireland met in Synod at Teltown in Meath, where Columba was accused of killing three thousand of Diarmit's men. After a trial *in absentia* he was excommunicated.

Later on, the Synod revoked their decision. But Columba, now humble and penitent and grieving at the outcome of his pride, would have none of their mercy. He passed sentence on himself, and that sentence was exile. Across the narrow sea, in the land of the Picts, he vowed to win as many souls for Christ as had fallen at Culdreimnhe. Once more the dove had subdued the wolf.

This is the story that the bookmen tell, and whether or not it's true in every detail, does it matter? Columba did come to Scotland. He did establish the Celtic Church in Iona. He *was* the greatest and most successful missionary the world has known. I feel inclined to call him the angry young man of his time; but I observe that instead of looking back in anger he always looked forward with love.

In the month of May, 563, he and twelve disciples left Ireland in a coracle, and as they sailed on towards the tangled coast of Dalriada, Columba made a homesick poem:

> How swift is the speed of my coracle,
> Its stern turned to Derry.
> My grey eye looks back to Erin,
> A grey eye full of tears.

They landed first, as I believe, in Southend, and the tradition is that Columba then travelled north to see his kinsman Congall, Chief in Dalriada of the Irish immigrant tribe called the Scots, who lived at Dunadd near Lochgilphead. From Congall he received permission to proceed to Iona, and there he finally landed, in a rocky bay still called in the Gaelic 'the port of the coracle'.

St Ninian had first brought Christianity to the Picts at the end of the fourth century. Like Montgomery after Wavell in the desert, Columba was about to take up what Ninian had started and go on to win the first great victory.

Having followed Columba from Ireland to Scotland I am now able to take a closer look at him in the context of my own country and my own people. Continuing the search for his magic, elsewhere than in Southend, I decide to visit Iona, by steamer from Oban.

The steamer is crammed with holiday luggage, with agricultural implements and day-old chicks, with bundles of pamphlets labelled 'Iona Community'. Crammed with people, too, white and coloured, ministers and priests, young men with cameras and open-necked shirts, old men with shepherds' crooks, young ladies with mini-skirts and stiletto heels, old ones with prim hats, teenagers with jeans and floppy hair, children in school uniforms.

As we sail out there's a glitter on the sea, and grey rocks go sliding past. There's singing and laughter and the music of guitars. I meet on the breezy deck a student from Nigeria.

I tell him that Iona was called by the Gaelic tribes 'island of my heart' or 'island of my love', and he tells me that in Nigeria there are places with similar names: 'the grove of my delight', for example, or 'the tender place of magic'.

Then we reach the island and visit 'the port of the coracle'. We see the gannets diving off-shore and the oyster-catchers wading at the edge of the white sands. We hear the larks and the peewits. We see kingcups in the marshy ground and irises along the banks of the stream. And, of course, bog myrtle everywhere.

I find a yellow St John's wort and tell my friend that this is Columba's flower, which the saint always carried inside his robe because of his admiration for John the Baptist, and which in Gaelic used to be called 'the armpit package of Columba'. He tells me that in Nigeria they also have flowers with magical names, one called 'the shield of the warrior' which is worn by men around their waists.

Then we turn and examine the ancient stones, the prehistoric meeting places of the Druids. From there we walk towards the modern Abbey, that lovely building restored by the devoted hands of ministers and divinity students, of architects and carpenters, of masons and doctors and musicians and poets; and, as we walk, I realise that though his love of nature was one source of Columba's magic, ordinary people confused and embarrassed by so-called new moralities were also his concern.

I tell my friend the story of Artbrannan, the old Pictish chieftain from Skye. Artbrannan was a pagan, but a kindly man whose life was blameless. He heard about Columba and his gospel of love, and before he died he said he'd like to become a Christian. So his men placed him in the prow of his boat, and when they reached Iona they carried him up the shore and laid him before Columba. Neither Columba nor Artbrannan could speak the other's language, but through an interpreter the saint instructed the old man, who believed and was baptised and was happy then to die.

In the shade of the Abbey we discuss the amazing breadth of Columba's personality.

Physically he was brave and strong, with a powerful voice which rang with authority. This is not to be wondered at. He was of royal descent, and had he not been dedicated to the Church he might have become High King of Ireland. He knew how to fight with sword and shield and had once commanded an army in battle. But he could also till the fields of Iona, help to build the 'cells' in which he lived with his disciples and was such a daring and skilful seaman that once, bringing urgent help to sick children in Jura, he sailed through the dreaded whirlpool of Corrievrechkan.

Morally he was also brave and strong. Like David Livingstone thirteen centuries later he travelled among savage tribes, with only the Cross as a talisman. He confronted the Druids on their own ground and by sheer force of character gradually won them over. He rejected the old idea that the gods were remote and cruel and in his own life demonstrated that religion is bound up with ordinary things.

My friend harks back to Columba's love of animals, birds and flowers, his delight in watching the colours of a sunset over the Atlantic. And as I nod agreement I remember another story.

When Columba was a boy he was often headstrong and selfish. At Moville College in Ireland one of his teachers was Gemman, the poet. One day, walking by the riverside with Gemman, he spotted a trout and bent down to catch it.

'Are you hungry?' said Gemman.

'Not in the least,' said Columba.

'Then why do you want to catch it? If you take it from the water it will die.'

'I only want to find out if I *can* catch it.'

'Ah,' said Gemman, 'so you'd kill the poor creature, just to satisfy your curiosity? How would you like it if God stretched down His hand and killed *you,* just to find out if He *could* kill you?'

I indicate to my friend that Columba, having learnt his

lesson, showed his love in a practical way. What may have been the first animal dispensary in history was in Iona, where he and his disciples gave medicine to sick lambs and injured birds. Not long ago, I point out, the newspapers made a big story about a crane with a damaged wing which made a temporary home in Kintyre. In Iona, fourteen hundred years earlier, there was a crane with a broken leg, and Columba cured it and sent it happily on its way.

He loved the wild things but he also loved children. It was about a child that he wrote:

> O conscience clear,
> O soul unsullied,
> Here is a kiss for thee.
> Give thou a kiss to me.

He gave women an honourable place in society. Ignoring a social structure in which women were regarded as chattels, he raised them high on a pedestal of reverence, reminding men of the dignity of motherhood as exemplified by Mary. In Iona a lonely girl in labour called for him, and he came and held her hand and prayed for her to Christ, 'who', as he said, 'was himself a partaker of humanity'.

He was rough and tough. He was gentle and kind. He was a warrior and a worker. But behind it all he was a poet. He wrote homesick poems about his beloved Ireland. He wrote gay songs which he sang lustily in the company of his disciples, because he always enjoyed a *ceilidh*. And he wrote this:

> Why is there pain at the heart of a song—
> Beauty that bleeds in the sweep of a hand on a harp?
> Why do I search, always in vain,
> For the home of my soul?

> Under the sun dark is my way.
> Under the moon haunted I go
> By the longing that cries from the heart of a song,
> The sorrow that pleads from an old man's eyes.

I wonder, as my friend does, if it was the travail of spirit
which inspires a poet that is the most important clue of all
to the magic of Columba. Because, come to think of it,
there's no lasting satisfaction, no triumph, no beauty without pain.

But there is also magic in travel and adventure, and
Columba enjoyed plenty of that.

He composed a prayer for travellers:

> Life be in my speech,
> Sense in what I say,
> The bloom of cherries on my lips
> Till I come back again.

He leaves behind a picture of himself in shoes of hide and
a homespun robe belted at the waist, 'traversing corries,
traversing forests, traversing valleys long and wild', wield-
ing his *cromak* as he marches with chosen disciples into the
savage land of the Picts, bringing with him the new gospel
of love and reverence for all men.

What was probably the most difficult but also the most
successful of his journeys was to the headquarters of King
Brude of the Picts. It took him along the rugged western
shore of Loch Ness, where he and his two companions saw
the monster, then up and across through the forests and dark
glens to the open settlement which is now Inverness. The
legends still flourishing about this historical conference, this
'summit talk' between a Christian leader and a pagan king,
prove that Columba was not only a saint but also a statesman, a clever and astute man of the world.

My friend asks a question concerning King Brude, and I
reply that though historically little is known about him I
have a mental picture of a friendly, sharply intelligent young
man with a sense of humour.

There is the story, for example, of how Brude first tested
the quality of Columba and his disciples by asking them a
series of questions.

'Tell me,' he said to Congall, 'what is more numerous than grass?'

And Congall replied: 'The dew-drops, your Majesty.'

'Excellent!' said Brude. 'Now, Kenneth,' he went on, addressing the second disciple, 'what is whiter than snow?'

And after only a little hesitation, Kenneth answered: 'The bloom of childhood, your Majesty.'

'Ah, yes, fair enough,' said Brude, 'though a trifle philosophical for my taste. But now, Columba, for you the hardest of all riddles. What is hotter than fire?'

In a flash Columba answered: 'A hospitable man when a stranger comes and there is nothing to offer him.'

At which the King laughed loudly and ordered a great feast to be prepared for his guests.

The story goes on to tell of how, as they feasted, Brude showed a keen interest in what Columba and his disciples had to say about Christ, even though Briochan, the Archdruid, was naturally suspicious and wanted to send them away.

Then the King had an idea. 'Columba,' he said, 'you argue that Christ is more powerful than the gods of the Druids. Briochan disagrees. Will you accept a challenge?'

'Certainly, your Majesty!' Never in his life had Columba refused a challenge.

'Very well.' Brude smiled at him. 'Briochan says that out there on Loch Ness he will summon up a storm of wind from the north. He says further that if you and your friends can sail a boat against it, he will then begin to believe in the power of this man you call Christ.'

Next day the storm bore down, and the waters of Loch Ness were flecked with white. As they climbed into the boat, Congall and Kenneth were frightened by what appeared to be Druid magic.

But Columba only laughed. 'This is no magic!' he said. 'From the furrowed clouds in the sky last night, anybody could have forecast a strong wind from the north—even Briochan!'

'But Master,' said Kenneth, 'can we sail against it?'

'Dear Kenneth,' replied the Dove, who had once been nicknamed the Wolf, 'haven't we often sailed past Corrievrechkan, close-hauled into a gale? Come now, hoist the sail, you and Congall! With God's help we will now show those ignorant landlubbers what Christian sailors can do!'

And so they cast off and tacked skilfully against the squally wind that roared down from the mountains. Watching from the shore, Brude slapped Briochan on the back. 'You see, my dear Archdruid, they sail against the wind! Their magic is stronger than yours! Mark well my words. Columba and his friends will remain here as my guests, to tell me more of Christ.'

This is not the traditional way of telling that story: it is a version I contrived for the benefit of my down-to-earth Nigerian friend. Adamnan, that devoted public relations officer, calls 'sailing against the wind' a miracle and makes it account for the fact that King Brude eventually allowed Columba to preach the gospel throughout Pictland. But Adamnan was as ignorant of seamanship as Brude and Briochan, and my friend, with his wide knowledge of what the psychological approach can accomplish among a primitive people, agrees with me that the whole incident, far from being a miracle, was probably a first-class publicity stunt conceived by Columba to impress his host.

But what's wrong with publicity, especially when you have something good to sell? The truth remains that Druidical influence among the Picts began to crumble under the influence of Columba's message of co-operation, neighbourliness and love.

In 574 this message bore further fruit. The Scots in Dalriada came to an understanding with some of the Pictish tribes, and Aidan, then Chief of the Scots, was elected the first King of a united Scotland. The crowning ceremony was performed in Iona by Columba. I remind my friend that Aidan was a direct ancestor of our present monarch and that the Druidic Black Stone on which he sat during his coronation is almost certainly the same Stone of Destiny on which the Kings and Queens of Great Britain are still crowned in Westminster Abbey.

In his old age Columba's missionary journeys became less numerous. Younger disciples took up the torch, travelling north into the farthest islands and south to Lindisfarne in Northumberland. He himself settled down to a domestic routine in Iona.

Though quiet, this routine was a busy one.

He and his monks held religious services every day. They studied languages: Latin and Greek and the Gaelic they spoke in common with the Scots. They practised the arts of writing and illuminating manuscripts, and this was a constant task, because all the churches founded by Columba on the mainland had to have service books.

They studied the stars, and, as the Archdruid Briochan found to his cost, they were all great navigators and sailors. They sang songs which they wrote themselves. They became experts on herbs and various medicines, and their monastery was a centre for both human and animal aid.

They grew barley on the *machairs* and had a seal-farm which provided oil for their *cruiskan* lamps. They built boats and fished, and from sheep's wool they made cloth for their robes. They made parchments for their manuscripts out of sheepskin.

They attended to pilgrims, first washing their feet in the manner of Christ, then providing them with hospitality in the guesthouse. Their food was barley-bread, milk, fish, eggs and sometimes mutton.

They were a humble band of brothers, owning everything in common, sharing happiness and sadness in equal measure.

But even in this gentle environment Columba was never afraid to speak his mind. His disciples often felt the rough edge of his tongue, though none of them resented it. And in spite of stiffening muscles he continued to make occasional forays into the Hebrides.

I tell my friend about a visit the saint once paid to a
monastery on the island of Eigg, where two monks had been
acting in a spirit of rivalry, each one claiming to be a
better preacher than the other. They were paraded before
Columba.

'My friends,' he said, 'stretch up your right hands towards
heaven.'

They did so.

'Good!' said this formidable commanding officer. He
went on: 'I see one of you is slightly taller than the other,
but neither of you can touch that white cloud floating in the
sky above us. Now, get on your knees and pray for each
other and for the people in your care, and then both of you
will reach higher than the clouds.'

So the monks fell on their knees and, as the story goes in
the Gaelic, 'their prayers which used to stick in the thatch
now mounted like sparks of fire into the heavens. Ever after
that there was brotherhood between the two monks, and the
brotherhood of the monks made brothers of the people.'

My friend liked this story. He could tell me one which
was strangely similar about witch-doctors in Nigeria.

On the ninth of June, 597, at the age of 76, Columba died
quietly while copying out the thirty-fourth psalm. The last
words he wrote were these: *They that seek the Lord shall
not lack any good thing.'*

Then he laid down his pen. 'Baithene must write the rest,'
he said.

And after the funeral Baithene, his disciple, began to
write the rest: *'Come, ye children, and hearken unto me, for
I will teach you the fear of the Lord.'*

There, under the wall of the Abbey, and not far from
where Columba lies buried, my friend and I contemplate
the many-sided character of this wolf who was a dove, this
saint who wore his halo at a decidedly jaunty angle. What
was the source of his magic? Leaving aside the factor of
personal magnetism, about which one can only guess, we
are forced to the conclusion that it must have been his care

for other people. People loved him because he loved them. After all, as any honeymoon couple can testify, love is magic.

But all this Beatle-copying 'magical mystery tour' has interrupted the story of children growing up in a country manse. Only when we became adults did Rona and my brothers and I begin to relate Southend's modern sociological condition to the legends of Columba. When we were young our main interest lay not in the community in which we found ourselves but in the individuals who lived in that community and their attitudes and behaviour as they affected us.

5

A View from the Manse

THEY say that ministers' sons—not to mention ministers' daughters—are always the worst. This is not necessarily true.

At one time, in a remote parish like Southend, before the BBC supplemented the *Glasgow Herald* as a guide to the manners and modes of larger communities, the sons of a minister tended to be judged on a different plane from other people. When Archie and Willie and I were adolescents we sometimes enjoyed half pints at the local inn, then went on to a dance and stayed out late with our current girl-friends. Afterwards nobody said anything about our drinking, dancing and necking companions, but we heard dark murmurings about ourselves: 'Och, the poor minister and his wife! Yon sons of theirs, leading the parish astray!'

It was hard living up to the image of the Manse and to the high ethical standards set by our parents—and Maimie. We had a sense of being at a disadvantage. Each of us *wanted* to be a Christian, but it seemed to us that the attainment of this was much easier for a farmer's son or a fisherman's son than it could be for a minister's son.

In any case, how does one define a Christian? This was a question we often asked ourselves, and it took us a long time to discover an answer. It turned out to be a vague kind of answer, suggested by—of all people—a Duchess.

She was a Dowager Duchess, her late husband having been George Douglas, eighth Duke of Argyll, who had served in the Government under both Palmerston and Gladstone. In her younger days she had been a private secretary with

Queen Victoria. Now, living in retirement at Macharioch House, one of the late Duke's numerous country 'cottages', she was an active member of the Padre's congregation.

She was accustomed to obedience and generally got it. On Sundays, Old Archie the beadle would never dream of ringing the church bell until he saw her Daimler approaching in the distance at a stately 20 m.p.h. And yet, when she at last came in and knelt to pray in the big Macharioch 'enclosure' in the gallery, we were always surprised to see how small and humble she looked compared with the numerous servants and flunkeys who sat behind her.

Ina Argyll, as she signed herself, was also generous, in a superior way. She put two lovely stained glass windows into the Kirk, one in memory of her husband, the Duke, the other in memory of Queen Victoria. And she did something else which appealed far more to us hungry boys: every Christmas she brought my mother an enormous turkey wrapped in strings of sausages.

She called at the Manse once a week. Sitting in state in the drawing-room, she invariably asked to see 'the boys'. We would be brought in like lambs to the slaughter. She would smile her stiff enamel smile and try to make us talk to her; but we were so numbed by her black dignity that as a rule the talk was painfully one-sided.

She had no children of her own, and I can understand now that she was lonely and perhaps as much afraid of us as we were of her. But human relationships were difficult between awkward schoolboys and a great dame who kept remarking to my mother: 'You know, my dear, as *Her Majesty* used to say . . .' The awful intonation she gave to '*Her Majesty*' sent shivers down our backs, in a way that the Padre's pulpit references to the Almighty seldom did.

But one day something happened to break the ice.

There we were in the drawing-room, seated around the fireplace, the Duchess and our parents making polite conversation, Archie and Willie and I grimly silent in our starched Eton collars. Suddenly we heard rumblings on the roof outside, and I remembered that Hughie the Sweep had said he would come and do the dining-room chimney that afternoon. But the rumblings were not above the dining-room: they were directly overhead. My brothers and I looked at one another with 'a wild surmise'; and sure enough, almost before the dreadful thought took shape, a great ball and brush came hurtling down the chimney to land in a cloud of soot at the Duchess's feet.

We felt as the Philistines must have felt when Samson brought down the Temple. The Padre's face took on its helpless look. My mother was ready to cry.

The Duchess took a moment to recover. Then she stood up and smiled. 'Poor Mrs MacVicar! But you mustn't mind. How lucky you are to have children who can enjoy the fun! Now, do let me help you clear up the mess.'

At clearing up she was a dead loss: she simply didn't know how. The Padre, of course, was equally useless. But when everything was over we did have an inkling of what he meant when he said: 'What d'you think, boys? She's not such a bad old Christian after all!'

Apart from being saddled with what we considered unfair ethical standards, we found other disadvantages in being the sons of a minister. For one thing, the Padre's stipend was so meagre that never in our lives did we get any pocket-money from him. For another, as we grew up, we found it difficult to discuss with our parents the problems of drink and sex. For a long time, until the incident of the bicycle plucked some of the scales from our eyes, we imagined they were too holy to know much about such earthy subjects. An entirely mistaken idea, of course. In an objective way nobody knows more about drink and sex than a minister, except, perhaps, a minister's wife.

But one tremendous advantage we did have. Living in a Manse, we met all kinds of people: Moderators of the Kirk, Duchesses, well-to-do farmers, erring youngsters anxious for advice, old age pensioners with papers to sign, tinkers with children they wanted baptised. We did our best to mix with them all, and I think we learnt not to be snobs—or anti-snobs—and to judge people on their personal merits.

On one remarkable night we had sleeping in the spare bedroom a visiting minister of the utmost piety and with us, in 'the boys' bedroom', a man we had found lying drunk and helpless at the back gate. Neither was aware of the near presence of the other, which, as Maimie said, was 'a God's blessing'.

I admit that we found our drunk man far more interesting than the minister. In the morning my mother and Maimie gave him aspirins, a good breakfast and some sharpish advice, and after that he often came to see us; sometimes, I'm afraid, much the worse for drink. He was big and tough —he had been a boxer in the Army—with a flashing temper when he hit the bottle, which was why he spent so much time in jail, convicted on charges of assault and battery.

His name was John Duncan, but we called him Big John. We would sit with him on the brown, lichened wall near the back gate of the Manse and listen to his stories, fascinated. He told us once that the first thing the old lags always asked for in jail was a New Testament. 'No' for the reason a minister's son might imagine, but because o' the rice paper. Just the job for rollin' fly cigarettes.'

He solved a number of our problems. One bright day in summer he took us down to the shore, and there, digging in the sand behind the target on the rifle range, he showed us how easy it was to find spent bullets, solid lead which we could sell to a scrap merchant. Another time he suggested that as we went round with the Padre on his ministerial 'visitations' we should ask people who had relatives abroad for foreign stamps, which we could sell to a dealer. It worked. It all worked like a charm. What a pity, with all our ingenuity, that neither Big John nor any of us ever became wealthy men!

He lectured us also on the subject of drink. He explained that he himself was an alcoholic. He couldn't help it, he said: it had to do with his chemical make-up. Others could take a drink and leave it, again on account of their chemical make-up. How right he was I have since discovered.

We all tried to reform Big John, and often he would stay on the waggon for several weeks. At such times he would be full of brash confidence, with big schemes to revive his electrician's business and make a fortune. Then another burst, another fight, another spell in jail.

Finally he was persuaded to join Alcoholics Anonymous. His first try was a failure. But he tried again and thirteen years ago became a confirmed teetotaller. I don't suppose any of us who can take a dram and leave it—and no great credit to us—will ever know how much that battle cost him. When he reappeared in public harsh lines were etched on his face, and nobody was afraid of his fists any more. He had become an old man, thin, pale and tired looking; but as a gesture of gratitude for his 'cure' he carried out free of charge—and by himself—a complete re-wiring of the lighting system in the Campbeltown Citadel of the Salvation Army.

He once said to me: 'What do they know about it, them that were never tempted? What do they know about winnin' a fight—and the satisfaction ye get after it?'

He died not long ago, aged 74, and was buried with full Salvation Army honours. Big John deserved it.

Because of the Padre's profession, death was a frequent subject of talk in the Manse. As children it used to frighten us. Not death itself, perhaps, but the question of what comes after it. Even yet this is a problem that worries me.

I wish I had the clear faith of old Hugh McEachran, who was one of my father's elders.

He rented the farm of Kilblaan across the river from the Manse, an irascible old bachelor with a red beard: the dead spit of Isaac in the Old Testament, we always thought. As Kirk Treasurer he looked after the collection on a Sunday, and the ha'pennies were as strictly accounted for by Old Hugh as were millions of pounds by the Bank of Scotland.

His family has flourished in Kintyre for many centuries.

The name McEachran means 'son of the horseman'; and it is interesting to note that the peninsula of Kintyre, of which Southend is the most southerly part, was described by Ptolemy, the Greek geographer, as *Epidion Akron*, 'the land of the horsemen'. In Roman times, it seems, the principal tribe in Kintyre was called *Epidioi*.

As small boys, we spent as much time as possible with Old Hugh. In the spring we joined the squabbling, worm-greedy gulls in the wake of his double-furrow plough, slipping and staggering and dirtying our boots among the polished earth and asking him naive questions about the farm, to which he usually replied in monosyllabic grunts. In the autumn, as he cut his corn, we helped him to do running repairs to his new-fangled binder, and for this we were sometimes rewarded by his grey-haired, work-bent sister Flora with huge 'dollar' biscuits thumb spread with butter and containing hunks of acid-tasting home-made cheese.

It was not from embarrassed parents or teachers or by means of arty-crafty films at school that we learnt about sex. Our education in this field began at Kilblaan, where, without comment from either the Padre or Old Hugh, we watched, occasionally, a travelling stallion serving one of the Clydesdale work-mares or, more frequently, a panting Ayrshire bull doing his duty by a smugly acquiescent cow.

We discovered that sex, like death, is a basic fact of life with which we must come to terms; and I think we were lucky to make the discovery so soon. I think we were lucky also to have had wise parents and friends who allowed us to make it in an honest, realistic way. Nobody ever tried to 'shield' us from sex, and thank goodness for it. As we grew up we learnt for ourselves that instant sex, as practised by a couple intent only upon selfish gratification, is often attended by physical revulsion and a host of psychological dangers. But we learnt, too, that untrammelled sex between a man and a woman in love can be among the most beautiful and rewarding experiences that life can offer.

c

My boyhood friend, Professor George Maurice Carstairs of Edinburgh University, created a furious press argument a few years ago when he stated in his Reith Lecture on BBC radio that charity is more important than chastity. I could never see why such an argument arose. To me his statement was self-evident. Chastity is a part of love. Without love chastity could not exist.

But all that is another story. My subject is Old Hugh and his attitude to the basic facts of life, including sex and death.

He had wanted to be a ship's carpenter, but his uncle had needed his help on the farm. He had done his duty, there-fore, and stayed ashore. Though never particularly keen on 'ploughing and sowing and reaping and mowing', he loved to build a cart or repair a threshing mill. Many a time we acted as his apprentices while he planed and chiselled and puffed through his beard and told us yarns about tidal waves and shipwrecks. Afterwards we would all troop into the big kitchen, with its uncovered cement floor and strings of dried cod hanging from the ceiling, and he would bark at his sister: 'Gi'e the weans a bloody biscuit.' He had no idea he was swearing, nor did we consider that he was. It never sounded wrong, the way he said it.

His concept of justice, like that of many characters in the Old Testament, was inclined to be harsh. When a neigh-bouring farmer accused his collie of the heinous crime of sheep-worrying, Old Hugh wasted no time. The law of the countryside had to be upheld. It also had to be seen to be upheld. He upended a cart, therefore, put a rope round the dog's neck and hanged her from one of the shafts.

Every afternoon at four o'clock he came to the Manse. His excuse was that he had to collect his mail, which the post left with us. At one stage we thought he was sweet on Maimie; but with considerable violence of both tongue and knuckly hand Maimie herself soon put that idea out of our heads. We began to realise that what he really came for was to forget the farm-work for a while and to speak with our parents—and with us.

As a rule we met him in the yard on his arrival, and invariably his first words were: 'Any signs o' the bloody post?'

One day in May, when hail showers and frost had blackened the shaws of his potatoes, I said to him: 'You must be pretty worried about your crops, Hugh?'

He growled in his throat. 'Look up the Book o' Genesis, boy. Chapter 3, verse 22. That'll gi'e ye the answer tae that.'

I looked it up and read: 'While the earth remaineth, seedtime and harvest, and cold and heat and summer and winter, and day and night shall not cease.'

During the last war, the *Britannia* was sunk off the West Coast of Africa and my brother Willie, her third officer, went missing for three weeks. During those weeks Old Hugh was in the Manse nearly all the time, not saying much, just being there. In his gruff way he would tell my mother: 'Dinna fash yersel'. He'll be in a life-boat, sailin' west for Sooth America. The trade winds, ye ken. He's a sailor: he'll be a' richt.' The day the telegram arrived to say that Willie and a boatload of survivors had landed in Brazil, Old Hugh was there in triumph: 'What did I tell ye, wumman? I kent fine he'd be a' richt!'

When the *Bismarck* was being hunted by the British Navy, Old Hugh took a keen interest in the whole operation. He appreciated that my mother, with four sons in the war, would also be interested and did his utmost to keep her up to date with the news. My parents had no radio set, but Old Hugh had one—a Heath Robinson effort constructed mainly of wood and piano wire—to which, during this period, he listened all day and all night, except when he was rushing across to the Manse with the latest information about the chase. In the morning, with some friends of hers, my mother was waiting for a bus at the Manse gate. Suddenly she saw Old Hugh approaching, blowing through his whiskers like a seal. Pushing everybody else aside, he came close to her: 'It's on the bloody wireless, wumman! She's doon! She's doon!'

Not long after this Old Hugh took ill. He was sick for some time, and at last he knew he was going to die.

One night the Padre sat by his bedside, and they talked and said a prayer together.

My father was amazed by his courage and stoic calm in the face of death. 'Hugh,' he said, 'I'm glad you're not afraid.'

The old man looked up and managed to smile. 'Feart, minister?' he said. 'Why should I be feart?'

Most of the older folk we knew as children are now gone. But we can never forget them, because we learnt something from them all. In the main it was something good, though swear-words and illicit cigarettes and the easiest methods of poaching a salmon came into it, too.

One thing we learnt was that a person's value cannot always be judged by his attendance at the kirk or by his holy demeanour on appropriate occasions.

There was Alec Soudan, for example, a member of the Padre's congregation but a backslider as far as the church was concerned. He spent most Sunday mornings looking after his collection of 'wee linties', the canaries and finches and other small birds which filled his house with their singing; and when this pleasant chore was completed he usually went across to the inn for a pint. (On a Sunday this used to be against the law. But in those days, in a country place like Southend, what the law didn't see the law didn't grieve about.)

There came a Sunday morning, however, when Alec entered the deserted bar and, to his dismay, found a brand new barmaid from Glasgow behind the counter. He eyed her with suspicion. 'I'll ha'e ma pint,' he ventured at last.

Pencilled eyebrows went up. 'Are you a *bona fide* traveller?'

'Naw!' said Alec, with indignation. 'I'm a gairdener frae Macharioch!'

During the first war he served for four years as a private

soldier and was 'over the top' four times. He was wounded in the face and patched up with an artificial jaw, which, he told us, was made of silver. This interfered with his speech a little but not with his enjoyment of life.

As a jobbing gardener he was invariably honest, inclined to underestimate rather than overestimate the hours he spent on overtime. Some people laughed at his 'innocence'. But I have a theory that the 'innocents' of this world are usually the happiest.

Alec was supremely happy with his gardening, his 'wee linties' and his Sunday pint. He had green fingers. He was 'sib with nature', as the saying goes, and when he looked after a garden flowers bloomed that had never bloomed there before.

He caught his 'wee linties' in the wintertime, tempting them with corn under a riddle and then, with a long string, jerking away the stick that held it up. He transgressed all the laws of man and nature, of course; but his idea was simply to bring the birds home to look after them and talk to them, until summer came and life was easier and he felt they would appreciate their freedom. Then he let them go, swearing volubly as he did so in order to hide his sorrow at losing them.

I remember Alec coming in from the road to look at some rather nice carnations which my wife was cutting in the garden. The soil around Achnamara, the bungalow I built in Southend when Jean and I got married, is notoriously sandy and barren, but for some obscure horticultural reason carnations thrive in it.

Alec surveyed the red blooms with admiration. He smelt them and held them up against the sun. 'Ay, missus,' he said at last, 'growin' in poverty an' fit for a show! Is nature no' wonnerfu'!'

Another of our friends was Barbara Jordan. Her married name was Mrs Neil MacCallum, but everybody in Southend knew her simply as Barbara. At one time she lived in a cothouse at Brunerican, the farm where Jean was born. Eventu-

70 SALT IN MY PORRIDGE

ally, however, on being allocated a new Council house in the village, she became our daily help at Achnamara.

She seldom went to church. On one occasion Jean did persuade her to attend a musical service, but her comments afterwards would have shocked the Padre had we chosen to tell him. 'Och, it wasna bad,' was her verdict, 'though I could ha'e been daein' wi' a wee cup o' tea at half-time. An' yon solo aboot Jerusalem! I'd far raither it had been *Scots Wha Ha'e!*'

She was always happy and full of optimism. She loved sentimental songs and stories, though invariably they made her cry. She cried also at christenings and at weddings— and, of course, at funerals. But the tears vanished as quickly as they came, and it was often disconcerting to be offering her a hanky one minute and to be assaulted the next by shrieks of laughter as she told some ribald tale concerning the dear departed.

In her younger days she worked as a milker at Brunerican, morning and night every day, in return for the cothouse and half-a-crown a week, plus milk and butter and eggs. Even when she was old, heavy and stiff she did occasional work in the fields, shawing turnips or gathering potatoes. But as long as Barbara got her 'wee cup o' tea' every half-hour or so, she was as happy as a lark. Her great interest in life was children. She had none of her own, but scores of youngsters in the parish had cause to love and bless 'Auntie Barbara', my own son Jock among them.

When another baby was expected in the village, and it appeared as if Barbara might be called in yet again to help the busy mother, her habit was to complain bitterly about the prospect. But when the baby arrived she would carry him in her shawl, and her face would beam when she met someone on the road: 'Och, isn't he an awfu' nice wee wean! Ye canna droon them, can ye?'

In her own humble way she went to endless trouble in caring for her children, hobbling through rain and wind to bring fruit or sweets or calf's-foot jelly to any who were ill.

She remembered their birthdays, and still remembered them when they grew up.

One day she went to the Post Office for her pension. She used most of it to pay a bill at the shop and was left with three half-crowns in her purse. But on the road outside she met three young mothers, each with a new baby in a pram, and when Barbara arrived home she had exactly nothing in her purse. Fortunately, she had so many self-styled 'nieces' and 'nephews' that the rent of her Council house was never any real problem.

When Barbara died, some years ago, I said to a neighbour of hers: 'So she's gone. We'll miss her, poor old Barbara!'

'What's poor about her?' he said. 'She'll get a big welcome where *she's* goin'.'

He was right, of course. I just hope they've remembered the 'wee cups o' tea'.

When my brothers and I were being sent off to a children's party—at Macharioch House, it might be, or at one of the big farms—my mother's last words usually were: 'Now, boys, remember you're the minister's sons and try to behave like gentlemen.' Hours later, when we returned, with ties askew and white Eton collars smeared with jam, bleeding perhaps from cuts sustained in an unseemly scuffle, we always felt that we had failed her.

It worried us, this question of what constitutes a gentleman. Instinctively, however, we recognised a gentleman when we saw one and were often surprised to discover that he didn't wear a top hat or speak with a posh accent.

One of the greatest gentlemen we knew was the Colonel, who wasn't a colonel at all but a retired gamekeeper, thin and tall, with a long lugubrious face like his own spaniel's. But when he bowed to the Duchess and her companion outside the church, or paused to have a word with Dan and Jamie, the roadmen, or got off his bicycle outside the Manse to speak to us boys, not as a superior being but as our equal, then his face would light up with a charming smile which

embraced everyone in a conspiracy of happy respect and
affection. His manner to his own wife, a small, dumpy
woman with a sharpish tongue, was exactly the same, and
they were a devoted couple.

The Colonel, of course, had his weaknesses.

He liked his dram, for example. He loved a 'big night' at
the Inn. Even with a full cargo, however, he remained the
gentleman, finding some difficulty with his consonants, perhaps, but none at all in keeping an upright stance, both
physically and morally. His influence at such a party was so
compelling that the behaviour of the whole company,
though naturally extremely happy, was always impeccable.

But the weakness which endeared him to us most of all
was his habit of telling plausible, yet highly dramatic stories
in which he himself figured as the hero. Our favourite was
his tale of how, as a young apprentice joiner in Paisley, he
had once played for St Mirren against the mighty Glasgow
Rangers.

He played as an amateur, he told us, and on this occasion
as a last-minute substitute for the St Mirren goalkeeper, who
had been taken ill. Goggle-eyed, we listened to his description of the game. We lived through his nervous fumbling of
the ball at the beginning, his gradual access of confidence.
The Rangers' forwards came thundering in—we could
almost see and hear them—and some of the Colonel's saves
were out of this world. But we knew that the great climax
had still to come, like a story in the *Boys' Own Paper*.

One minute to go, the score at nothing, nothing. Suddenly,
out of the blue, a foul by the St Mirren right back. The
referee pointing to the spot. A penalty for Rangers.

The Colonel looked down at us, on the hearthrug by his
chair. 'A great hush fell upon the crowd,' he said. 'I
crouched there in the goal, knowing well that I alone stood
between St Mirren and relegation from the First Division. I
said to myself, "Watch his feet, man! Watch his feet!" The
Rangers' centre-forward came pounding in, as if meaning to
shoot to my left, but at the last moment I saw him shuffle

his feet and flung myself to the right. The ball thudded against my chest and I held it with a grip of iron. Then the whistle went. I had saved St Mirren.'

We breathed again.

'And do you know,' he concluded, modestly, 'that day I was carried shoulder-high from the park at Love Street.'

I don't suppose the Colonel's name, which was Neil Mac-Kay, is to be found in the St Mirren records: there were some who classed his stories as 'a lot of lies'. But his lies were never malicious, never hurtful: rather the reverse. They were told, I firmly believe, because he knew they gave pleasure to others as well as to himself.

He spoke ill of nobody. He had consideration for his fellow-men and respected their dignity. If this is not the mark of a gentleman I don't know what is.

6

Campbeltown Loch, I'm glad you're not Whisky

ON passing our 'qualifying' examinations in Southend School at the age of about eleven, we all, one after the other, went to the Grammar School in Campbeltown, ten miles away.

When the time came for Rona, Kenneth and John to go, special school buses had begun to operate; but Archie, Willie and I all had to cycle into town on a Monday morning, live in lodgings during the school week and cycle home again on a Friday evening. Though we had splendid digs in Glebe Street with Mrs Rankin, an understanding young matron with a son of her own, it was remarkable how often we felt the need of a clean collar, which meant cycling to Southend on, say, a Tuesday evening and then back to Campbeltown early the next morning. Lured by the prospect of an unscheduled night at home, happed in comfort by my mother and Maimie and hero-worshipped by younger members of the family, we were deterred neither by rain nor by wind, and if our home-work suffered we bore the brunt of a teacher's anger and thought it well worth while.

Archie developed into a powerful footballer and won a soccer blue at Glasgow University, while Willie and I became athletes and competed for money at the many Highland Games held annually in all parts of Argyll. We had 'good legs', as they say, and considered this to have been the result of so much hectic cycling in our school days. (The Padre maintains that the MacVicars *always* had good legs.)

I went to Campbeltown Grammar School in 1920. Twenty-one years later I found myself at Stirling Castle, in a

bare room with a polished wooden floor. Wearing battledress, I stood awkwardly at attention beside an oak table,
at the opposite end of which sat three high-ranking English
officers. They were members of a board engaged upon the
selection of trained recruits suitable for transference to an
Officer Cadet Training Unit. All in all, they were exceedingly pleasant gentlemen compared with the sergeants and
sergeant-majors whose iron authority I had endured for the
past six months.

The one in the middle had a port-wine complexion and a
fluffy grey moustache. He asked the inevitable question:
'And now, what was your school?'

'Campbeltown Grammar School, sir.' I saw blank, not to
say puzzled looks spreading across three faces; but with un-
characteristic presence of mind I went on: 'You remember,
sir, it is mentioned in Boswell's *Life of Johnson*.'

The old boy with the fluffy moustache swallowed, turned
a little pinker, then suddenly guffawed and slapped the
table: 'Of course! Slipped me memory for the moment. Ha,
ha! Damn fine school, eh?'

His fellow board members picked up their cue and laugh-
ingly shook their heads. How on earth had they, too, experienced such an extraordinary lapse of memory?

From then on the interview went like a bomb. The son of
a parson, the author of thirteen works of fiction to date *and*
a former pupil of the famous Campbeltown Grammar
School, I could have become an officer there and then as far
as that board was concerned. Bless them all!

Campbeltown Grammar School is indeed mentioned in
Boswell's *Life*, though in an oblique way. James Boswell
was one of the counsel engaged by John Hastie, headmaster
of the school, who, in 1767, was dismissed from his post by
Campbeltown Town Council for cruelty to his pupils and,
unsuccessfully, took his case for reinstatement as far as the
House of Lords. The *Life* records Johnson's opinions on
the case; and in transcript some of Boswell's pleadings bear
obvious marks of the great Doctor's composition.

In fact, however, 'the Grammar' had little in common with an English public school. There was no segregation as between male and female, black and white, tinker's son and banker's daughter. I found myself in a new world, and the soft puppy-fur of a sheltered life in Southend was quickly rubbed away. Smoking, drinking, swearing and sex were no longer objective and vaguely amusing. I was now subjectively involved, and the experience made me gasp like a bather in a cold sea. Fortunately I didn't drown.

I discovered I was good at English. Our austere but basically sensitive English master, Alexander ('Sandy') Banks, described the fabric of my early essay-writing as 'decidedly woolly'. In the following six years, however, he did everything he could to encourage my ambition to write.

I was good at Maths and Science as well, not because I had any latent talent in this direction but because George Hutcheon, head of the department, had a personality more forceful than most. During school hours he belted us with a strap dreaded from Tarbert to the Mull of Kintyre and, after school hours, taught us with dour Aberdonian charm how to play cricket.

We played teams from naval ships visiting the harbour, teams of former pupils, teams from Kiel School, which is now in Dunbartonshire but was then housed in a mansion in Southend. Though bordering 50, 'George' played in and captained our XI himself, always at No. 5 in the batting order and at cover-point in the field. Out of his own pocket he paid all our travelling expenses and often provided a picnic tea as well.

On a Monday morning, as we entered his room, he would be standing solemnly by his desk. On the blackboard, for the benefit of our classmates, he would have inscribed in chalk a record of notable performances in Saturday's game:

MacQueen 5 for 22
Wylie *not out* 28
MacDougall *b*. Carter 25
MacVicar *b*. Simpson 0

'George' would make no verbal comment, nor would a comment—or even a smile—be allowed in the class. After a few seconds he would take a duster and wipe the board clean. Then, as a beginning to the day's work, he might put a poker-faced question, 'McVicar, define zero', which required an equally poker-faced and mathematically sound reply.

Though eventually I passed all my Maths examinations at School and University I still can't count up to ten without using my fingers. But I did learn something from a long, enforced involvement with the subject. 'George' taught us to set out theorems as follows: *Given, Required to Prove, Proof, Conclusion.* It is the perfect formula for the composition of an article or a story, and I have been using it with profit for more than forty years.

For French we had Jenny Bain, a darling lady who could produce, for our benefit, any number of delectable Mademoiselles from France. For Latin we had an unfortunate victim of shellshock. Both classes were dreams of delight for young hooligans released from the stern disciplines of Sandy Banks and George Hutcheon. We put carbide in inkwells, bumped our elbows against flimsy partitions, pinched the girls sitting in front: not for nothing did we read Billy Bunter and other popular school comics. In short we created merry hell and endured frequent beltings from Rector Cunningham ('Old Connie') for the sake of the gorgeous fun we were having. Had marijuana been in fashion I'm sure we would have tried to smoke it.

Only once did I feel mortified in receiving the belt. On a desk in one of the rooms, during a particularly boring spare period, I had thoughtlessly carved the outline of a yacht, with the initials *A.M.V.* in the mainsail. The class which followed us was composed entirely of girls, some of whom noticed my masterpiece and informed their teacher. The teacher immediately summoned the Rector, and the Rector summoned me. In front of the giggling girls—one of whom was Jean, who is now my wife—he administered seven

overarm swipes, three on my right hand and four on my left,
which raised huge bruises on both my wrists. Then, to complete my misery, he remarked as we left the room that he
would be sending my father the account for a new desk. He
had no such intention, of course, but for weeks I went in
fear of the arrival at the Manse of that account. 'Old Connie'
was a brilliant exponent of the art of psychological punishment.

My closest mates were Davie Watson, Alan MacDougall,
Tom Wylie and Hamish Taylor. They were known, respec-
tively, as 'Sherlock Holmes', 'Big Alan', 'The Wily Bird'
and 'Boskers'. My nickname was 'The Drake', because I
had—and still have—a large bottom; and several girls on
whom from time to time I cast lascivious eyes were, in con-
sequence, nicknamed 'The Duck' (pronounced *Juck*).

We chewed gum like the reckless heroes we admired in
the picture house (tickets for two in the 'flea-pit', sevenpence
and fourpence). We wrote notes to each other and passed
them along under the desks. Sometimes these notes concerned cricket or football, sometimes a night's fishing in
one of Big Alan's family boats, sometimes the raiding
of an apple orchard up by Castlehill. Sometimes, if life
was becoming stale, they signalled a bout of partition
bashing.

Once, right under Jenny Bain's oblivious eye, Watson and
I played Cupid, though at the age of sixteen, with acne-
raddled faces and short trousers exposing hairy knees,
neither of us looked in the least like a god of love.

Alastair MacMillan, who sat immediately behind us, had
developed a crush on a girl in the class called Barbara.
Alastair, however, was painfully shy and panted for her only
at a distance. In a mood of warm consideration for my
fellow man, therefore, I composed a poem in French, which
Watson, who possessed great skill in copying handwriting,
wrote down on a sheet of paper—above the signature 'Barbara'—as follows:

> *Alastair, mon cher,*
> *Avez-vous*
> *Un peu*
> *D'amour*
> *Pour moi?*

We pretended to receive it from Barbara in front, then passed it back and watched with pleasure 'the red tide flooding o'er his cheek'. Unfortunately, unknown to us, Barbara had no crush on Alastair—it turned out her secret passion was for Watson—and that night we had to rescue her from his amateur clutches down by the life-boat shed.

No, Watson didn't become a master forger. He was brilliant at Maths and is now, understandably, a prosperous chartered accountant practising in Perth.

For Art we had 'Wee Dolly' Smith, from whom we learnt all the intricacies of light and shade. Only once did she experiment with a free art session. On this remarkable occasion we were all directed to draw an animal of our own choice and given an hour in which to do it. The resultant 'zoo' was weirdly indescribable. Boskers, whose home was a farm in Southend, produced a hen with four legs, which rendered Wee Dolly speechless and, from that day on, put paid to free art as far as our class was concerned.

For all those unskilful in drawing and painting, it may be encouraging to note that Boskers eventually commanded a battalion of Argylls during the last war, became a successful farmer and is now an Honorary Sheriff Substitute and the Vice-Convenor of Argyll County Council. On the other hand, I once gained a prize for Art, and I also, much to my secret astonishment, became an Honorary Sheriff Substitute.

During the six years my brothers and Rona and I commuted between Southend and Campbeltown we learned a great deal, in school and out of it. We grew tougher and more self-reliant, both mentally and physically. And we developed an affection for Campbeltown second only to our affection for Southend.

In the early twenties, when I was at the Grammar School, the Royal Burgh of Campbeltown appeared to be a much busier place than it is today. Often, with my mates, I stood at the Old Quay Head and saw and heard and smelt it all.

Fishing-skiffs were close-packed in the inner harbour, gulls squabbling in the bare forest of their masts. On the sea-front raw-skinned and oilskin-aproned herring gutters flashed their knives and exchanged unladylike remarks with the fishermen. At the Old Quay the graceful, red-funnelled Campbeltown steamer loaded screaming pigs, barrels of new potatoes and boxes of cured herring. At the New Quay, factory coal from the pit at Machrihanish crashed into a puffer's hold out of dangling trucks lifted bodily from the narrow-gauge railway.

In the outer harbour lay the big ships: herring-buying Klondykers from the Continent and grain-ships from the Black Sea transporting Russian barley to the distilleries.

Horses and carts lumbered on to the weigh-house scales with loads of coal from Ayrshire, loads of wet, steaming draff from the distilleries (bought by farmers for cattle food) and loads of lime from neighbouring quarries. In the western sky black smoke hung above the distilleries. From Trench Point the clang of hammers gave body to a symphony of clattering steam-winches, rumbling lorries, strident fish-salesmen.

There was a smell of salt and tar and fish, with the delicate aroma of malt to sweeten it.

Today the prospect is different.

The ancient Celtic Cross, whose origin remains a mystery, has been moved from the centre of Main Street to the Old Quay Head. I take a seat on its stepped base and survey scenes and sounds that are far more peaceful.

The weigh-house is still there, used occasionally by coal lorries. But in the inner harbour the fishing skiffs are few, elbowed into corners by the brightly painted dinghies of the Sailing Club, by rowing-boats for hire and by pleasure-craft preparing to carry sightseers to the famous cave picture on Davaar Island.

Inside the sheltering arm of the New Quay lies the waiting, watchful life-boat, *City of Glasgow II*, paid for by subscriptions from the generous citizens of Glasgow, with next to her, a fishery protection vessel, sleek, grey and hygienic-looking. At the Old Quay squats a black nuclear submarine at rest during an Atlantic exercise, her off-duty sailors playing leapfrog on empty bollards. Where horses once pulled heavy loads there stands a row of turnstiles, clicking busily as summer visitors embark from a Clyde pleasure steamer.

The outer harbour is bare, a sparkling expanse of blue water whose buoys are occupied only occasionally by visiting yachts, though on one fabulous occasion in August 1958, the *Britannia* and her naval escorts used them all and prideful pinnaces brought Her Majesty the Queen and H.R.H. the Duke of Edinburgh to the steps of a crowded and beflagged Old Quay, where Captain Hugh Mac-Shannon, the harbourmaster, had his finest hour.

The sea-front, where lusty girls used to eviscerate their fish, now displays a pattern of graceful pavements and well-trimmed grass, decorated with slot-machines for milk and long rows of fairy-lights to compete with the dazzle from two cinemas. Cars and articulated lorries purr on the round-about, and the western sky is clear, except for the daily plane flying into Machrihanish from Glasgow's Airport at Abbots-inch. On Kinloch Park, where fishermen used to dry and repair their nets, children do acrobatics on the swings and young holidaymakers play football and court their girls.

There is a smell of salt from the sea and a thin acridity of petrol, but the scent of the flowers around the Cross is not outdone.

Before and after the last war depression and unemployment have been endemic in the town. Distillery owners, facing competition from new plants in the Highlands, found

their profits at risk and in a panic closed down all but two
of more than twenty local stills. To illustrate the extent of
this disaster, it may be pointed out that about seventy years
ago 6,500,000 gallons of whisky were stored in bond in
Campbeltown, enough to make every man, woman and
child in Britain happily drunk at the same time. To make
matters worse, the universal slump in shipbuilding between
the wars put an end to the Yard at Trench Point, which, in
the forty-six years of its existence, produced 116 vessels,
some of more than 4000 tons.

As a schoolboy I saw the last big ship, the *Akenside*, being
launched at The Trench in January 1922. Then, more
recently, the coal pit at Machrihanish became uneconomic
and it, too, was closed down; while over the years, owing
to the dwindling popularity of the herring as an ingredient
in our modern diet, accompanied by the soaring cost of
boats and nets, the fishing industry has steadily become
smaller.

Miraculously, however, Campbeltown's population of
7000 citizens, like the citizens of many another small town
in the west of Scotland, have learnt to adapt themselves
to changing conditions. Admittedly, the town's present
economy is based substantially on summer visitors and on
the prosperous farming community by which it is surrounded. But there are other compensations. Two distilleries remain viable. A large creamery producing butter,
lactic casein and condensed milk provides a solid wedge of
employment, while a few years ago an English firm took
over the derelict shipbuilding yard and has now begun to
build and repair light craft both for business and pleasure.
A clothing factory and some small food factories have
been established, and the fishing fleet, now small but highly
efficient, makes a profit not only out of herring, white fish
and clams but also out of prawns for the fashionable scampi
market.

Indeed, the folk of Campbeltown are now, on the whole,
better off than they have ever been, though a hard core of

some two hundred unemployed is an evil blemish on the picture.

This may appear to be a paradox, because in the legendary good old days Campbeltown was reputed to be the richest town in Scotland for its size. At that time, however, its wealth was concentrated in a few pockets. 'Big hooses' were built, mostly with whisky money, along Kilkerran, Askomil and the High Road; but in Fisher Row and Bolgam Street were impoverished slums, and beggars grovelled in the gutters to drink wash from the overflowing stills. Now many of the 'big hooses' are divided into flats, some have become boarding houses, one has been gifted to the Church of Scotland as an Eventide Home, another is a Maternity Hospital. But the slums are almost entirely gone, and the Town Council's sustained housing programme has brought comfort and dignity to the mass of the townsfolk. Today there is no gulf between the 'gentry' and the 'working classes'; and it may be a sign of the times that the so-called 'Gentleman's' Club in Main Street has acquired a bus-stop near its door.

Campbeltown's cultural life is richer, too. Its famous Gaelic Choir, winner of the Lovat and Tullibardine Shield at the National Mod on fifteen occasions, has been employed in films and by the BBC. Its amateur drama clubs compete with the best in Scotland. Its Music Club, Antiquarian Society and Junior Agricultural Club all have large memberships.

Its footballers and athletes train in Kintyre Park, and there is ample scope for its badminton and bowling enthusiasts. Its golfers learn the game at Machrihanish and on the links of Dunaverty at Southend. And if Southend takes full pride in having nurtured a Scottish Champion and Curtis Cup player in the person of Mrs Belle Robertson, a recurring British Police Champion in David Galbraith and a Scottish Girls' Champion in Isobel Wylie, a little of the credit for their prowess may be granted to Machrihanish and Campbeltown.

The town's churches are well attended and, in my opinion, would be even better attended if they were fewer. In these days of sprawling new towns, when some much larger communities have no church at all, it seems incongruous that Campbeltown should have eight different congregations, four Church of Scotland, one Free, one United Free, one Episcopalian and one Roman Catholic, with the Salvation Army and Plymouth Brethren working on the side.

A fine new Grammar School was opened in 1969, almost incredibly handsome and efficient as compared with the tatty, rambling old buildings which housed my generation. It has a staff of nearly forty teachers and a senior roll of about six hundred pupils. Its library would take Sandy Banks's breath away. Its baths, showers and playing-fields would do the same for George.

The town's activities are reported in the *Campbeltown Courier,* about which, in view of the fact that it gave me my first and only salaried job, I will have more to say later on. Established in 1873, its circulation is currently around 5000; and in the past few years—another sign of the times— its advertising revenue has considerably increased.

Nevertheless, despite a surface gloss of well-being, it seems to me unfortunate that Campbeltown's principal export should continue to be people, though this is a situation reflected in many small Highland towns not so fortunate as Fort William with its pulp mill and Invergordon with its chemical works. Campbeltonians can be found in every corner of the world: in England—particularly at the steel mills in Corby—in Canada, Rhodesia, Australia and New Zealand, on the prairies of the United States and amongst the crews of far-journeying ships. They are known as soon as they speak, because their accent is unmistakable, a curious blend of braid Scots, Gaelic and the brogue of Northern Ireland.

Some years ago I scripted a BBC film about my father— *The Old Padre* it was called—for which I also did the commentary. When it was shown in Australia and Tasmania

I had scores of letters from people saying how thrilled they had been to hear the Campbeltown accent again.

The exiled Campbeltonian's dream is to come back; and if he is of the true stock he generally does come back.

7

The Picture in the Cave

CAMPBELTOWN folk are undemonstrative, as befits descendants of lowland tradesmen and farmers; but the Irish strain is there to give them a twinkling humour, and the Highland strain is there, too, making them generous and hospitable. During my six years at the Grammar School I received kindness from both rich and poor. I was made welcome at the 'big hoose' of ex-Provost Mitchell, the distillery owner, at the crowded manse of the Rev. George Walter Strang, minister of the Lowland Kirk, and at the dignified mansion occupied by Sheriff MacMaster Campbell.

Ex-Provost Mitchell and his daughter Helen often conducted me on fascinating tours of their Rie-clachan Distillery, which, however, no longer operates. Jeanie Strang, the minister's elderly daughter, sometimes made me wealthy with the gift of half-a-crown, which invariably led to an orgy with my mates at Leo Grumoli's ice-cream establishment in Hall Street. (We composed an appropriate verse: 'Ice-cream cools a belly on a warm day; but hot peas warm a belly on a cold day.') Sometimes I attended the court presided over by Sheriff MacMaster Campbell, a notable Gaelic scholar and one of the founders of the National Mod. He was big, stout and jovial, with a sibilant stammer. Confronting a poacher in the dock, he would fume and splutter and promise hellish punishment. Then, in a voice of thunder, his judgment would be delivered—a fine of five shillings. No wonder the fairies often left salmon, pheasants and hares on his doorstep.

I was also made welcome in humbler homes in Fisher

Row and Bolgam Street, where old men who had been distillery workers, like Sandy McIntyre, told hair-raising tales
of drunken fighting in the streets, and younger fishermen,
like Andrew Brown, gave vivid accounts of attacks on their
skiffs by basking sharks. But Duncan Newlands was—and
continues to be—my hero and favourite storyteller.

Duncan is a smallish man, stockily-built, and, like most
seafaring Campbeltonians, has a liking for double-breasted
navy blue suits worn with a dark blue polo-necked jersey.
When I knew him first he was spry and quick. He is now in
his mid-seventies, and a form of rheumatism, the aftermath
of many stormy nights spent at sea, has slowed him down.
But he still thinks as fast as he did when the life-boat under
his command was in danger; and, to use a simile of his own,
his memory is 'as clear as a kitten's eye'.

His clean-shaven face, round and reddened by the
weather, is ordinarily serious, which provides a background
for occasional deadpan humour at some innocent's expense.
When he finds congenial company, however, and his silence
turns to animated talk, a broad smile lights up his face, like
sunshine on a cloudy sea. With children he is happiest; and
he is proud of having trained, privately and at night school,
a number of young men who are now in the merchant navy
and in the life-boat service.

Like many of his contemporaries in Campbeltown, he has
earned a living doing many things, as deck-hand, stevedore,
fisherman and boat-owner. When work in the town was
scarce he never once applied for the dole, because in his
code this would have been a bitter humiliation.

He is brash, outspoken, quick to use the forthright language of the sea. Strangely enough, however, one of his pet
aversions is alcohol, and though he never stinted the life-
boat rum ration when it was required, he himself has always
been a teetotaller. 'But I'm a sucker for the ginger wine,' he
says. (He means the ginger wine which is kept in all life-
boats for those who prefer it to rum.)

When he retired in 1962, he had been a member of the

crew of the Campbeltown life-boat for forty-one years and coxswain for eighteen. He had taken part in exactly a hundred services and helped to save more than three hundred lives.

What may have been Duncan's greatest rescue took place several years after I got to know him. It illumines his character better than any story I could tell about him.

On a grim, dark night in March, 1946, the *Byron Darnton* of Baltimore, an American liberty ship of 7000 tons, went aground on the island of Sanda, three miles off the Southend coast. I remember the night well, because it was a Saturday and I had been playing golf. Darkness came down early, with a gale blowing up from the south-east and the sea rising.

News that the *Byron Darnton* required assistance was transmitted to Campbeltown by the Southend coastguards at 11.10 p.m., and Duncan and his regular crew of seven took the life-boat out: a reserve boat as it happened, the *Duke of Connaught*, a 45-foot Watson whose motors were known to be temperamental. In addition, she had no radio-telephone, no mast-head signal lamp, no searchlight.

On this occasion a life-boat was certainly an urgent necessity. Having gone ashore inside the notorious Boiler Reef, directly under Sanda Lighthouse, the liberty ship was in considerable danger of being broken up by pounding seas, and on board were fifty-five passengers and crew.

On Duncan's first attempt to get alongside, the *Duke's* rudder was smashed, and his crew had to spend hours fixing an emergency tiller. By the time they got the job finished it was morning, and the storm was growing worse, with sleet and snow whipping amongst the spray.

At this stage, Jim Russell, the farmer on Sanda, volunteered to give Duncan the benefit of his intimate knowledge of the island's coast. About mid-day, with incredible courage and skill, they took the *Duke* in towards the wreck, through a narrow passage in the Reef.

Now it was a race against time, because a large crack was

widening in the ship's side. Boats were quickly lowered from the *Byron Darnton,* and the women survivors were lifted carefully into the life-boat. Men came scrambling down the davit falls.

Finally the Captain reported to Duncan that only four of his crew remained in the ship. By this time the sound of tearing metal in the great hulk had become continuous, and Duncan was edgy. 'Where the hell are they?' he demanded.

Captain King was apologetic. 'I sent them for a case of whisky,' he said. 'A reward for your magnificent crew.'

Duncan declares he was 'struck dumb'. He appreciated the Captain's kindly thought, but if the whisky came aboard he had a vision of about sixty coxswains in the *Duke*—not just one—and the service was only half completed.

So, as he says, he 'thought quick'. When the men appeared at the rails above he shouted to them not to drop the case into the life-boat because this might damage her, but to let it fall instead into the water. They obeyed at once. Then Duncan made a show of trying to catch the case with a boat-hook; but surreptitiously, as the men slid down the davit falls, he nudged it hard against the ship's side. It broke up and sank, and in spite of some fancy American language that was the last of the whisky.

As the *Duke* steamed through and away from the Boiler Reef the *Byron Darnton* broke in two, 'with a noise like thunder'.

On this service Duncan and his men spent nearly eighteen hours at sea. Their pay, per man, was £2 16s 6d, and they didn't even get a dram. Duncan himself was awarded a clasp to his bronze medal, while for his initiative in helping to keep the *Duke*'s engine going in the emergency, Duncan Black, the bowman, received the thanks of the Royal National Life-boat Institution inscribed on vellum.

The survivors were loud in their praise of Duncan. One of them said to him: 'After this you'll never need to work again, Scotch cox'n!' But from that day to this he has heard nothing more from any of them, and the owners of the

Byron Darnton have made no contribution whatsoever to the funds of the RNLI. Nevertheless, Duncan looks back on this rescue with great satisfaction, because fifty-four lives were saved, a record for the Campbeltown station. In any case, as he has so often told me, he 'aye gets a kick out o' helpin' other folk'.

One of his quieter adventures occurred when I was at school and he had a boat of his own for hire.

On a Sunday afternoon in summer he was approached on the sea-front by an old man wearing a cloth cap and working boots, with a weeping wife in tow. The old man was clearly much upset. He stammered out that they had missed the cruise steamer back to Ayr and that he was almost certain to lose his job as a gardener if he failed to report for work the next morning.

'What will you charge to take us across in your boat?' he asked.

Duncan thought for a minute. The old couple looked so poor, and so anxious and unhappy, that he couldn't bring himself to quote the full fare. 'Pay me for the fuel,' he suggested. 'And give my two apprentice lads a quid apiece.'

The old man looked even more unhappy. 'I don't have that much money on me,' he said. 'But if you could wait I'd send it on to you.'

'All right, we'll wait.' Duncan tried to cheer him up. 'And even if the money never comes, we'll not go to our graves missing it!'

When they reached Ayr, after a pleasant crossing, Duncan told the two old people that a bus to take them to their destination could be found in the Square; but they seemed oddly reluctant to leave the boat. By now everybody was ravenous, so Duncan asked one of his lads to go ashore and buy three fish suppers, to set them up for the return journey. 'You ought to buy the same for yourself and your wife,' he advised the old man.

'I wish I could.' His passenger had a longing look. 'The trouble is, I've only got fourpence in my pocket.'

As Duncan says, he might have been a sucker, but what could he do? He raised the order for fish suppers to five and afterwards gave the old man the price of two bus fares.

He never expected to see the money again. But over the next few months the old man paid back every penny, in postal order instalments.

When telling this story Duncan always adds a footnote. 'In this life,' he says, 'you've got to trust in folk.'

My admiration for Duncan—and, indeed, for all life-boatmen—began when I was at school in Campbeltown. It has stayed with me ever since.

Life-boatmen may be fishermen, farmers, miners, lawyers, publicans, shopkeepers, but they all have something in common—a warm humanity and a gallant ideal of service. The RNLI pays them thirty shillings for the first two hours in the boat and seven and sixpence an hour thereafter. Such earnings are taxable, and there is no overtime. But in spite of the discomfort, in spite of the fear that always nags at them during a service, I am convinced they would do the job for love. When they hear the detonations of the two warning-maroons and see the green stars bursting in the sky, nothing stops them racing for the life-boat shed, because they know that somewhere out there, in the wild, black weather, a ship is in danger and human beings like themselves are in distress.

When I am troubled by the various activities of certain long-haired pop musicians and other leaders of a small sick society, I take refuge in thinking about the life-boatmen, and soon the world seems sweeter.

I have scripted for the BBC more than a dozen features about the life-boat. I have also published two books on the same subject: *Life-boat—Green to White,* a novel for children, and a documentary entitled *Rescue Call.* For all these projects I was well paid. But the job of work which brought me most satisfaction was the Life-boat Appeal I broadcast on television in 1966, for which, appropriately, I wasn't paid a penny, not even travelling expenses.

Duncan, of course, figured largely in that programme, and
if he is proud of being the coxswain of the Campbeltown
life-boat, I am equally proud of having done this small service for a voluntary Institution which is undoubtedly the
best of its kind in the world.

Vessels enter Campbeltown Loch by a narrow passage
between Trench Point and the northern side of Davaar
Island, which is marked by two buoys called the Millmore
and the Millbeg, or, locally, the Winkies.

Frequently it looks as if a boat could enter the harbour
by way of a channel on the southern side of Davaar; but as
a number of amateur yachtsmen and submarine commanders have found to their cost that channel is obstructed by
a sandbank, the Dhorling, which even at high tide is only a
few feet under the water. At low tide it is possible to walk
dry shod from the mainland out to the island.

I remember once, as a boy, being among a party of
visitors bound for Davaar in Duncan's boat. As we chugged
out through the Loch we were so low in the water that even
at ebb tide the Dhorling was invisible. Suddenly a figure
appeared in the distance, walking towards the island as if on
the water. A wee Glasgow man in the bow was galvanised
by astonishment. 'Hey, mister!' he exclaimed to Duncan.
'There's a fella daein' Jesus oot o' a joab!'

Having explained away the apparent miracle, Duncan
went on to describe the other 'miracle' we were about to see
on the island.

According to geologists, Davaar, like Ailsa Craig, is the
hard core of an extinct volcano. Over millions of years
the sea has cut deep caves in the brittle rock. And in
one of these caves, in 1887, something was found which
made headlines not only in Campbeltown but all over
Scotland.

On a summer evening a crowd of young fishermen landed
on Davaar and began to explore, shouting and throwing
stones to hear the echoes in the caves. Entering one large

cave they were surprised by an unexpected glimmer of colour. Then, as their eyes grew accustomed to the dim light, they saw it on the wall, a huge picture of Christ on the Cross. Terrified, they turned and ran, back to their boat and back to Campbeltown, where they spread the news.

Some thought it was a miracle and that the picture had blossomed on the rock-face of its own accord. From all parts of Europe and America people began to make pilgrimages to see it, pilgrimages which still go on. A few years later the truth came out. In the spring of 1887 a Campbeltown artist called Archibald McKinnon had a dream. He had never been to Davaar, but in his dream he saw a cave on the island with a magnificent picture of the Crucifixion inside. Next day he went to Davaar and to his astonishment found the cave exactly as he had seen it in his dream. At once he resolved to create a picture on the rock-face, so that his dream might come wholly true. He began visiting the cave in secret, walking out across the Dhorling at low tide. No one saw him going or coming—or perhaps busy people simply paid no attention to the wanderings of a poor and unimportant artist—and in six weeks the picture was finished.

This was the story told by Duncan on that long-ago trip to Davaar. In 1934, when he was living in retirement in Cheshire, Archibald McKinnon came back to re-touch his picture. He was then eighty-four years old, but while the work of restoration was going on, he always walked across the Dhorling as he had done forty-seven years before.

In 1963, as a labour of love, the picture was again re-touched, this time by J. J. McAnally, the Scots artist, who was then an art master at the Grammar School.

I was working on the *Courier* when Archibald McKinnon returned to his native town. I asked him if he had made a good living as an artist. He said: 'I was only an artist when the mood was on me, and that mood didn't come very often. I earned my bread and butter as an art teacher.'

It seems that the picture which made him the most money

had an Irish setting, the subject being an old woman rounding up her pigs at feeding time. 'I put a devil sitting on the
last wee pig's tail,' he said.

But the picture in the cave, from which he made no
money at all, this was his masterpiece.

8

Ministers, Are they Mortal?

AMONG well-intentioned but often sorely bewildered ordinary folk, what is the popular image of a minister of religion?

I think there are three images. The first is of a saintly, silver-haired figure, worthy of sentimental affection and regard but so remote from mundane reality that only a few are encouraged to approach his ivory tower with problems they want to discuss: problems, for example, of drunken driving, of marital unhappiness, of questionable business deals. The second is of a black crow, skirling black theology from the pulpit, a sour critic of Burns Suppers, of golf on a Sunday afternoon, of drama, drink and dalliance—and, inevitably, of dances in the Village Hall. The third is of a slightly ineffectual young man playing the guitar to his dwindling Youth Club.

As children growing up in a Manse, we had an opportunity to study the genus 'minister' at first hand. (Apart, I mean, from our own father, who was—and is—a study in himself!) In those days, between the wars, it was the custom for a parish minister to invite a colleague to assist him at his Communions and other special services. In our case, the visiting minister always stayed at the Manse. My mother would bake soda scones for him and put a bottle in his bed and warm his slippers at the dining-room fire. Then, after the thanksgiving service on the Sunday evening, as a special treat, she might serve for his supper a noble salmon taken from the burn by unconventional means. During the weekend our parents and their guest would talk. We would listen and watch and form our conclusions.

Visiting ministers came in all sorts and sizes—missionaries, moderators, fiery evangelists, the 'dreich' and the 'gey dreich', those who insisted on holding family prayers before the morning service and those who were so nervous about preaching that they breakfasted on aspirins.

There was the eminent church historian who found himself at twelve o'clock on a Saturday night in the middle of an exciting rubber of bridge and who sighed with relief when the Padre rose and stopped the clock until the rubber had been decided and the holy Sabbath could officially begin.

There was the minister from nearby Campbeltown who laid on a show of magic for us in the drawing-room and to my great delight used me as his assistant and rubbed the ashes of burnt paper on my arm and made Rona's name come up on it in big black letters.

There was the saintly innocent who thought that the letters BTM referred to a military decoration, which caused Willie to swallow his soup the wrong way and be sent from the dining-room in disgrace.

There was the handsome young minister from Glasgow who played football with us on the Saturday afternoon, and on the Sunday, because Maimie was away, helped my mother wash the dishes, calling her *mo graidhe* ('my dear' in the Gaelic) and at night played the piano and sang her favourite songs. Him we loved, in spite of the cigarette ash he scattered everywhere.

There was also the stout divine from the far north who preached hell-fire for those who drank to excess and then had three helpings of rich plum-pudding at lunch, leaving my mother with none, and who later called her 'a frivolous creature' because she gathered some flowers on the Sabbath afternoon. Him we hated, which shows what a lot of little pagans we were.

From our peculiar point of vantage, what was our image of a minister? We didn't have one. At an early age we came to the conclusion that ministers are the same as ordinary men, well-intentioned but often sorely bewildered, good,

'The Padre' 1970

Angus MacVicar

'Black House', North Uist, where the Padre was born

Manse of St Blaan's, Southend, where we were brought up

'A focal point in Southend is Dunaverty Rock'

The salmon fisherman's hut, Southend

Left: J. J. McAnally retouching the cave picture on Davaar Island

Below: Campbeltown from the air, with Davaar Island and the Dhorling at the mouth of the loch

Wreck of the *Byron Darnton* on Sanda Island, March 1946

European survivors of life-boat no. 7, s.s. *Britannia*. Third Officer
William MacVicar is seated, third from left

Left: 'Ever so coy'—our wedding in 1936

Opposite above left: Last photograph taken of my brother Archie

Opposite above right: The Padre with my mother only a year before she died

Right: My sister Rona at the National Gaelic Mod, 1948

Below: My mother with Rona, Mima and John, 1940

'MacVicar preach-in': *l to r* Willie, John, Esme, myself, Jean, Isabel, Kenneth; *seated*, Nina, the Padre, my mother, Jock

The view from my study window: Dunaverty Rock and Sanda Island

bad and indifferent. Some we liked: those whom we knew instinctively could understand our sinful problems and help us work out the answers. Some we detested: those whose reaction to any pleasurable human activity was always a nasty 'No!'

But we did have a fair idea of what makes a *good* minister. An old Doctor of Divinity from North Uist once said to the Padre: 'You cannot be a good minister, Angus, unless you love your people with all their faults. And you cannot be a good minister, either, unless your people love *you,* with all *your* faults.'

Which is a saying to be pondered over, not only by ministers.

I think children are remarkably shrewd about grown-ups. They are not always attracted by people who make a fuss about them, nor are they necessarily repelled by others who are gruff, outspoken and apparently dictatorial.

For example, one of the visiting ministers we always liked to see was the Rev. George Walter Strang, whom I have mentioned before. He was strong and stocky, with a sharp little grey beard and, at times, a highly irascible manner. He never played down to us; he was never 'smarmy', which was our private word for the gushing kind. His questions about our school work and games were always asked in a man-to-man kind of way, and this pleased us.

He died more than forty years ago, but his name is still a legend in Campbeltown, where he ministered to the Lowland congregation for most of his life. He was such a straight-shooter that were he alive today I have a notion his nickname might be Wyatt Earp. So honest that he could never play a part, he said and did what he thought was right and damned the consequences.

He loved a game of golf and on one occasion played truant from a meeting of Presbytery in order to play a challenge match with his bosom crony, the local Roman Catholic priest. The wrath of the Presbytery fell upon his head,

D

but he spoke out squarely in his own defence. 'It was a lovely day,' he said, 'ideal for beneficial exercise, and surely the health and strength of a minister is important to his congregation. As for playing with the priest, he is a very nice man. We may differ in the details of our religion, but we both believe in God.' Finicky, ecumenical problems never worried George Walter.

His ideas on the ordinances of public worship could be described as conservative. One day the Presbytery was considering an Assembly Report on new and unconventional methods of presenting the good news to the people. After a while George Walter could stand it no longer. 'What are they trying to tell us?' he demanded. 'For thirty years I have preached in my church the gospel of Christ and the Ten Commandments. What more do they want me to do? Stand on my head in the pulpit and waggle my feet in the air?' Which, as can be imagined, brought the discussion to a quick and even hilarious conclusion.

As he grew older he became more than a little absent-minded. Once he forgot a wedding date. A messenger came rushing to the Manse door to remind him, and in some distress he threw on his hat and coat and stumped rapidly down the street to make amends. Bursting into the house, he saw the young couple, the best man and the bridesmaid standing in a row before him. 'Tell me,' he panted, 'which of you is the father of the child?'

It is not only because of his irascibility and absent-mindedness, however, that George Walter is so warmly remembered today. Throughout his life his passion for golf was as nothing compared with his passion for the welfare of the poor in his parish. Sometimes he was criticised for spending too much time with people who didn't actually belong to his congregation. He dismissed such criticism with a piratical snarl.

One Christmas he preached a sermon about a notorious slum in Campbeltown called the Wide Close, and what he said in that sermon still echoes in the folk-lore of Kintyre.

A wealthy distiller was so moved by it that he paid not only for the demolition of the Wide Close but also for new houses for the slum-dwellers in another part of the town.

No one knows how much George Walter himself gave to the poor; but it must have been as much as he could afford. His philosophy was simple and direct. As we often heard him say to the Padre: 'What's the good of praying with people unless you fill their stomachs first!'

When the Padre told us that Willie Webb was coming to the Manse we thought it was the famous Scottish football referee. We were mistaken. Our guest was Willie Webb, the tinkers' padre, who in his day has kept the peace among crowds of people as excited as any football fans, in Scotland, in England and in Europe.

He is small and self-effacing; but in the pulpit he seems to grow in physical appearance and spirit. We recognised at once that Willie Webb is a phenomenon and that occasionally his frail body is possessed by unnatural strength.

He is not a minister, though at one time, as an ordained missionary, he was employed by the Church of Scotland to look after the spiritual health of Scottish tinkers. He followed them wherever they went, under the sun or in the cold and the rain, learning their private language, preaching to little groups in straw-filled tents. He helped them load their barrows, and carried the delicate children on his back and offered a helping arm to old men lame with rheumatism. He prayed with the women in labour and held their hands as St Columba did fourteen hundred years ago.

For the past thirteen years, helped and encouraged at first by the late Hugh Redwood, he has been a freelance, travelling all over Britain and the Continent, preaching to tinkers and gypsies, attending their rallies in France, Germany and Finland, steadfastly and insistently sharing with the nomads his knowledge of the love and reality of Jesus.

Not long ago he came to live beside us in Kintyre; but his

Dormobile is his real home, and the speedometer on its dashboard records the kind of mileage done by a busy commercial traveller. He still follows the tinkers, arguing, settling quarrels, feeding the hungry and healing the sick, unembarrassed by squalor, disease or disbelief, equally unembarrassed by the gifts of wealthy people who see in him an agency for their charity. A supremely happy man.

The mystery of Willie Webb is that without an income of any kind he has no financial worries. I myself have often prayed for money, with the result that the next day I received yet another batch of overdue accounts. But Willie Webb *believes*; for him prayer works. I know for a fact that when he wanted a Dormobile he went down on his knees and asked God for it, and a few days later it appeared in a garage bearing a note: *For Willie Webb*. To this day he has no idea where it came from.

His accent is more suited to a tinkers' conference than to a garden part at Holyrood House, and it is unlikely, therefore, that he will ever sound forth in Glasgow Cathedral or in St Giles in Edinburgh. (He knows this himself and has given me his permission to write about it.) His style of preaching is what might be called ultra-evangelical, but, to use a favourite remark of his own, it sure gives me a thrill. He regards Jesus as a personal friend. Like Don Camillo he talks to Him, there in the pulpit, and the answers come with a power that is almost frightening. With my intellect I may question some of Willie Webb's assumptions, but in my heart I am stirred and troubled.

His faith is absolute. 'Listen, folks,' he shouts, 'listen to what I'm going to tell you. Hugh Redwood had a cancer. They wanted to operate but Hugh Redwood said no, I will pray instead. And the cancer was cured—cured, folks, cured. I'm telling you, Jesus takes upon himself our infirmities and cures our sickness. Hugh Redwood knew, I know. What about you?'

The Rev. Kenneth McLeod of Gigha often stayed in the

Manse. The Padre and my mother considered him one
of their greatest friends.

One evening, at tea-time, we were enchanted when he
turned to my father and said: 'When we go to heaven,
Angus, I hope we'll find a place prepared for us, with a
notice on the wall, *Argyll and the Isles*. And I hope Mrs
MacVicar will be there, too, looking very glamorous and
baking scones to keep St Peter happy.'

He was small and thin, with a narrow brown face and a
black Victorian moustache, and his glistening, deep-set
brown eyes could shop gaiety and sadness, mischief and
compassion, all in the space of about thirty seconds.

At the age of twenty-two he was told he had consumption
and only a year to live. At all costs he must give up smoking.
Sixty-one years later, kippered with cigarette smoke, he died
peacefully and happily, with a lifetime of magic behind him.
'Only the good die young,' he used to tell us children, 'so
we're all right!'

He began as a missionary in the Hebrides, where he
preached to the people and listened to them singing in their
'black houses' and, like St Columba, shared their troubles
and their longings in his poems. Some of the stern, black
ministers shook their censorious heads and called him
Coinneach nan Oran, 'Kenneth of the Songs', in sarcastic
disapproval of his lightsome ways. Their conception of
religion was harsh and bleak. Kenneth's was different, as is
shown by my favourite among his poems:

Dance to your shadow when it's good to be living, lad.
Dance to your shadow when there's nothing better near
    you.
Dance to your shadow when it's sore to be living, lad.
Dance to your shadow when there's nothing better near
    you.

As a minister, he settled finally in Gigha, 'the last jewel
in the island chain of the Inner Hebrides'. Lying two miles

off the west coast of Kintyre, it has an area of less than six square miles, which makes it the smallest parish in Scotland. In 1923 its two hundred inhabitants built a new and lovely little church on *Cnocan a'Shuil,* 'the hillock of music'—the fourth place of worship to be erected on the same site in three centuries—and Kenneth became its first incumbent. I was there the day he was inducted to his new parish and watched him plant two rowan trees at the gate of the church, 'to ward off the witches', he told me, as solemn as a judge.

In general, the Gigha folk are farmers and fishermen, as modern and up-to-date as their Kintyre neighbours; but their domestic language is the Gaelic, and Kenneth was happy among them. During his long ministry there, with assistance from his friend Mrs Kennedy Fraser, he rescued hundreds of beautiful Gaelic songs from oblivion in the Hebrides. For one he wrote new words himself: *The Road to the Isles.*

I think it was his sense of fun—often completely unexpected—which endeared him most to his new congregation. One of the stories he liked to tell was about a commercial traveller who reached Gigha feeling sick and sorry for himself after a stormy crossing on the ferry from the mainland. When mine host at the hotel introduced the minister to him as 'the man who made *The Road to the Isles,'* all the poor traveller could say was: 'I wish to heck he'd made a road to Gigha!'

Among the young folk, for whom his bachelor Manse was always open house, he became especially popular. He never preached to them. He told them stories about Finn and Cuchullain and about the fairies who lived in the green knolls of the Hebrides. At times he was so carried away by emotion that he broke down in tears. His stories had no specific moral, but all were coloured by love and hope and faith in the goodness of people. If a boy confessed a sin to him, he would say with a twinkle: 'You know, I'm always suspicious of a man who never smokes or drinks or goes with a girl—and who likes cocoa!'

He loved to go to the General Assembly of the Church of Scotland in Edinburgh, not particularly on account of the Assembly but in order to meet kindred spirits and have fun. When he and the Rev. Dr George MacLeod of the Iona Community (now Lord MacLeod of Fiunary) met for the first time in a Princes Street restaurant, he waved aside the Padre's introduction: 'Don't bother, Angus. George and I have known each other for a thousand years!'

Once, at Assembly time, he invited the Padre and my brother Kenneth (then, as now, minister of Kenmore in Perthshire) to come and see him at his cousin's flat, where he was staying in Edinburgh. When his visitors arrived he was nowhere to be found. Then his cousin spotted a note on the tea-table in the living-room: 'Please give the MacVicars my apologies. I have been called away to an ecumenical conference.'

With her kettle on the boil, his cousin was mortified. 'Oh, damn that Kenneth!' she said. 'You never know for two minutes what he's going to do next!'

'You're right there!' came a voice from under the table, and Kenneth crawled out, laughing all over his face.

He was eighty at the time.

Kenneth MacLeod was in love with people. He was also in love with life, perhaps, in a way, because he lived his own on a lot of borrowed time.

Clergymen are distrusted, even by religious people, and only a minority are prepared to admit that a clergyman is a source of comfort in times of trouble. This was one of the astonishing conclusions reached by a national survey carried out by the Independent Television Authority. Organised by the Opinion Research Centre, the survey also found that only twenty out of a hundred people are in favour of moral problems being discussed on television by clergymen. It showed, too, that there exists 'a strong resistance to church services on TV' and that TV sermons are not popular.

Admittedly, these results were based on a sample poll of

little more than a thousand people aged 16 and over, pre-
dominantly English. But I believe they indicate a trend, even
in Scotland, where the image of the minister has steadily
deteriorated, especially since the last war.

In a period when the Church of Scotland allowed clerical
stipends to fall to mere subsistence level, there is no doubt
that some men lacking leadership and character were en-
listed in a ministry starved of recruits. But the situation has
now changed. Stipends are adjusted to the cost of living,
and a dedicated young man can *afford* to become a minister.
In any case, simply because it takes considerable guts to
preach Christianity in our modern permissive society, the
majority of clergymen are of necessity men of courage and
good will, eminently suited to the role of trusty friend and
comforter.

Why, then, does the image of a minister remain so poor?

I think television itself is partly to blame. When last, on
BBC or ITV, has a minister been portrayed who wasn't (a)
a well-fed pompous bore, toadying to the rich and powerful,
(b) a mental case, shrieking hell-fire in dark corners, or (c)
a hand-wringing, chinless nitwit?

This kind of cardboard characterisation is, of course, only
what might be expected from that dreary and uninspiring
travesty of drama, the Wednesday Play, which, as a rule,
shows people wallowing in every kind of perversion and yet
seldom admits that human nature can be kind and courage-
ous as well. But why should a series like *Dr Finlay's Case-
book,* which gives an otherwise honest and sometimes even
brilliant account of Scottish life and character, always seem
to knock the ministry? Its doctors, lawyers, farmers and
shopkeepers are sometimes good and sometimes bad, which
is fair and true to life. Why, therefore, should its ministers
always be bad? Or, if not actively bad, at least sycophantic,
time-serving moral weaklings? If doctors, lawyers, farmers
or shopkeepers got this kind of one-sided treatment on television their public relations men would utter such screams
as would shatter every eardrum in Broadcasting House.

One of the best public relations men Christianity ever had was Tom Allan. The Rev. Tom Allan, evangelist, organiser of the Tell Scotland Movement, minister of the Church of St George's Tron in Glasgow, was another welcome visitor at our parents' Manse, though by the time we came to know him most of us in the family were grown up.

While on holiday in Southend he often joined us on the golf course, where he played with the same joy and enthusiasm he put into everything.

Though a first-class golfer, he was willing to play with anybody, even a self-confessed duffer. In fact, I think the games he enjoyed most on Dunaverty were with two small boys from the village who operated with ancient clubs and tatty old balls fished out of the burn. As a rule the boys were shy and quiet with strangers, but with Tom, all the way round the course, we could hear them chatting and laughing. Sometimes they played in their bare feet, and when they did so Tom played in his bare feet, too.

Once I came across the boys outside the clubhouse, practising their swings with great earnestness. 'The first tee is empty,' I said. 'Off you go.'

They shook their heads. 'Waiting for Mr Tom,' they said, smiling with an eagerness they seldom showed.

But what Tom used to call his 'day of glory' on Dunaverty was when he had a hole in one at the fourteenth hole. I was among those playing with him, and afterwards we had the usual celebration. He made no objection to having a drink, but he himself would take nothing stronger than orange-juice. 'If I took one dram,' he said, 'I should be liable to take a dozen.'

This was part of his appeal. He knew what temptation was and could, therefore, speak about it not only with authority but also with understanding.

That night we talked about something beyond my experience, the fact of instant conversion. I am always suspicious of people who tell me they have been converted and seem to flaunt their piety and purity in my guilty face. It was different with Tom. Instant conversion had happened to him, but in his case I knew without question that it was true. I could see it in his eyes. As we talked he flaunted neither piety nor purity but did his best to explain that while for some conversion is like a blinding flash, to others it comes in a long slow process. 'It can be happening to you,' he said to us.

And then he told an extraordinary story.

After the last war, in Paris, where he worked with Intelligence, a great friend of his was an American colleague, a man he called Big Bill Campbell. Tom had been going the pace, living 'without the benefit of religion' as he put it himself, and Big Bill was anxious. Finally, after days of argument, he persuaded Tom to go with him to church; and that day Tom heard the negro singing *Were you there?* and a new life opened up for him.

Years later he was in New York, with his name in neon lights on the church he was going to preach in. On the Saturday evening, out walking with his wife, Big Bill Campbell saw the sign and went to Tom's hotel. The aftermath of war had caused Big Bill to lose his faith and give up the church, but he wanted to say hello to an old friend.

Tom talked to him. 'Come to church tomorrow, Bill. It can't do you any harm.'

Big Bill was reluctant; but after a while, 'for the sake of peace and for auld lang syne', he agreed.

Next day, as was his custom at the end of a service, Tom asked all those who had found renewed faith to come forward. Big Bill was the first to do so.

The wheel had turned full circle.

Tom Allan lived to help and encourage not only his many friends but all those with whom he came in contact. He worked so hard at doing it that in the end it killed him. But who can ever say he wasn't privileged?

The image of a minister? As I have already said, Rona and

my brothers and I never had one, but the ministers we have known—those we have known personally and those we have known in imagination, like Columba—most of them had a common attribute, an enduring love of people.

9

A 'Lisping Stammering Tongue'

In October 1926 I became an Arts student at Glasgow University. I was unimpressed by this five-hundred-year-old seat of learning.

The impersonality of its teaching and administrative staff was decidedly odd after the personal authority I had experienced in Southend and Campbeltown. I had no feeling, either, that my fellow students and I made up a close-knit community, ready to act and demonstrate in concert in any cause, good or bad. We arranged ourselves in a variety of cliques, the members of each clique having an introvert loyalty to one another and a disinterested lack of sympathy for anything or anybody outside this little world. As some naive characters on the modern 'pop' scene do, we offered lip-service to an ideal of harmony with the whole human race, but it was the harmony of others with *our* conception of life that we meant, failing to appreciate that harmony between young and old, rich and poor, artists and philistines, can only be achieved in terms of two-way traffic.

As it was, the 'medicos' had small truck with the law students, who existed equally apart from the 'engineers'. The Students Representative Council and their 'establishment' hangers-on looked down their noses at the Gaelic culture heroes of the Ossianic Society, while the lusty members of the Athletic Club eschewed the company of egg-head Conservatives, Liberals and Socialists. Nobody paid any serious attention to the 'divines'.

I was involved with two cliques.

As a member of the Athletic Club I played soccer in

winter and in summer took part in athletics at Westerlands,
the University Ground at Anniesland Cross, attaining no
great distinction in either. Once—and once only—I played
left back for the first Football XI and was sent off for
charging to the ground an annoying opponent and then
questioning the right of the referee to award a penalty
against us. Fortunately my brother Archie came along a few
year later and restored the MacVicar reputation by winning
a soccer blue. I enjoyed the company of other athletes, however, and felt good after a hard game of football on a cold,
wet December afternoon or after a training stint on a warm
evening in May. On those occasions we usually adjourned
to the pub at the corner of Park Road and Gibson Street
where the Padre and his friends had founded the Shinty
Club.

But it was as an inmate of the Students' Residence at 11
Oakfield Avenue that I got to know the real meaning of a
clique. (The word 'inmate' is carefully chosen, as I hope to
demonstrate.)

The Students' Residence, now divided up into residential
flats, was supposed to be for budding ministers, but it had
room also for medical and legal students, apprentice accoun-
tants and bankers and a few American, Swiss and French
transfer students. In my day it was run by a fragile, white-
haired but immensely determined lady called Miss Wood,
who loved her 'students' in spite of their frequently shocking
behaviour. Some of us got drunk, some of us made passes
at the maids, some of us drank coffee and ate chocolate
biscuits to excess at Hubbard's Tea-Room across the street.

Some of us once staged a revolution against the authority
of the head man, a former chemist studying for the Church.
When we barricaded ourselves inside the study, sustained by
bottles of beer, the police were called in, and only tearful
intercession by our friend, Miss Wood, saved us from
appearing in court. Thereafter the revolution was never
talked about beyond the confines of the Residence.

Were such an incident to occur today the chances are it

would become a nine-day wonder in newspapers and on
television, and in the end the Home Secretary would undoubtedly be held responsible. Sinister murmurs about the
birch and the cat, interspersed with whispers on how much
it was costing the country to educate such 'louts', would run
sibilantly through the land, and statistics would sprout on
front pages and in *Panorama* indicating a catastrophic
increase in delinquency and violence among students.

(I refrain from publishing the names of those involved in
the various ploys which took place in the Students' Residence, so as to avoid embarrassing a number of individuals
now eminent in the religious, medical and legal life of
Scotland.)

If I was unimpressed by the University, the University
was equally unimpressed by me. Charmed by that great man
Professor McNeile Dixon, I had no difficulty in passing the
exams in English, both Ordinary and Higher, though in my
Anglo-Saxon degree paper for the latter, in a misguided
flush of genius, I translated 'aetbrede' as 'wheaten loaf',
whereas 'aetbrede' means 'nevertheless'. I had no trouble
either with History, French and Moral Philosophy, but, lacking George to spur me on, I had to re-sit Maths, and it took
me three years to gain a pass in Political Economy. Laws
such as those proposed by Malthus and Adam Smith have
always seemed to me depressing and unrealistic. Sounding
infinitely wise in theory, in terms of human application they
are as irrelevant as *The Naked Ape* and other scientific sur-
veys to a young couple in love.

It was during summer vacations at the Manse that the
degree results used to come out. The Padre was unsympa-
thetic with my ignominious failures and showed it. My
mother was sympathetic but sad. Maimie scuttled in and out
of various rooms, muttering darkly about 'giving the poor
boy a chance'. The rest of the family kept diplomatically
quiet. It was a great relief to all concerned, therefore, when
at last, in 1930, my name appeared in the *Glasgow Herald*
as having graduated Master of Arts. In doing so I had

accomplished a minimum of work for a maximum of pleasure, and my stay in Glasgow, thanks to Carnegie's annual £10 and to contributions from the Kintyre Club, the Dundonald Foundation and Argyll Education Authority, had cost the Padre very little, though probably about as much as he could afford. Now I faced the prospect of putting lightsome pursuits aside and preparing in earnest for my life's work.

To the delight of my parents, who had always hoped I would become a minister, I enrolled as a divinity student. Their delight was transient. A few months later, after a brief brush with Hebrew, New Testament Greek and Comparative Theology, I gave up thoughts of entering the Church and said goodbye to the University. Why am I what we in Scotland call a 'stickit minister'? There are two reasons. The first, I suppose, is that I'm not as much of a Christian as I should like to be. The second is a story in itself.

One afternoon, when I was about four years old, I went for a walk with the Padre into the hills above Kilblaan. When we came back to the Manse I had a stammer. How this happened I have no idea. I didn't have an accident or get a fright. I just began to stammer.

Afterwards, at school in Campbeltown, it was a godsend. Sandy Banks, George and Jenny Bain seldom asked me questions which entailed long answers. If, for a moment, they did forget my disability and demand that I speak, I started to make a noise like a steam-engine in agony, whereupon a glazed look would come into their eyes and with gentle embarrassment they would request me to sit down again.

Of course, I put it on a bit. What schoolboy wouldn't, especially if it meant relief from too much strenuous homework? But I paid for my sins.

At the University, playing football and training for the hundred yards and the two-twenty, I got rid of my incubus, to a certain extent. I know now that the basic physical cure for stammering is the development of well-tuned muscles in the diaphragm, and I expect that the exercise did that for me. It was with a fair amount of confidence, therefore, that I decided to begin studying for the ministry.

In the Divinity Hall the question soon arose, when was I going to preach my first sermon? A close friend of mine was David Elder, who later went to Ghana as a missionary and now ministers in Sanquhar, Dumfriesshire. He was helping out in a church in the East End of Glasgow and after some persuasion finally made me promise to take an evening service there.

At first I was appalled. Then, being a MacVicar, I found that the idea of standing up in a pulpit and airing my views was becoming more and more attractive. I wrote what I thought was a marvellous sermon on the text, 'Faith without works is dead'. (I have since discovered that most young ministers begin with a sermon on the same subject.) Then I chose an appropriate praise-list and rehearsed what I was going to say, like an actor. 'Now's your chance!' I kept telling myself. 'Maybe you have a Moderator's breeches in your knapsack after all!'

But that Sunday evening, as I took a tram-car from the Students' Residence in Hillhead to the East End, I was beginning to feel not so much a Moderator, more a prisoner bound for execution. The tram-car swayed, the wheels went clanking over the points. I have a sick feeling in my stomach right now, even thinking about it.

Then the walk through the dark and the rain to the church, the cold vestry with the faded red cloth on the table, the silent beadle with the red, rough face whisking away the big Bible to place it solemnly in the pulpit before coming back like a jailer to chivvy me inside. The church itself, smelling of damp and varnish and inefficient oil-heaters, the scattered blurred faces waiting in the pews. And finally— finally the violent stammering with which I announced the opening psalm.

I got through it. Somehow I got through it. But that night my old man of the sea had a real ball. At the end of the service my faith was buried in the ruins of my works.

Afterwards an old lady who had sat and listened came to see me in the vestry. She stooped a little and wore a black shawl: I think she was the beadle's wife. 'Och, son, never you mind,' she said. 'Someday you'll have a good laugh about it.'

I haven't laughed about it yet. From that moment I made up my mind I was going to write instead of speak. Oliver Goldsmith had spoken 'like poor Poll' and gone on to 'write like an angel'. I could but try to emulate him.

Over the years, however, I have always tried to keep the muscles of my diaphragm in good condition. I have disciplined the temptation to escape, gibbering, from every invitation to speak on a platform, or on radio or television. By such means I have achieved an uneasy truce with my old man of the sea. But he still sits on my shoulder, nowadays not so much an enemy, more perhaps an awkward friend.

Why does anybody become an author? The reasons are complex.

To begin with, like an artist or a composer, he must have an urge to create something, a desire to present his views on a variety of subjects. This presupposes a certain amount of vanity, and there can be no doubt that vanity is a factor in an author's personality. The trouble is, as he becomes more and more involved in the work of authorship his vanity soon melts away in the heat of the many humiliations that beset him.

Then there is the luring knowledge that a successful author enjoys a large degree of freedom and independence. He is his own master; all he requires for capital are his own wits. He gets no subsidies, grants or other aids from the state and is therefore beholden to nobody. He can, in theory at any rate, take an afternoon off whenever he likes to play golf or to smell the flowers. In practice his freedom and independence are illusory. His own conscience and the desperate need to earn enough money to live are masters more authoritarian than any Hitler.

There is also the bait of easy money. He has heard—as I did—of men like James Hilton, who was paid £30,000 for the film rights of *Lost Horizon,* and like J. B. Priestley, who made a cool £50,000 from *The Good Companions.* He has visions of a mansion in the country, complete with butler and Rolls Royce. When the day-dream is overtaken by reality his disillusionment is traumatic.

That, then, is the picture, with a stammer an added incentive in my own case. An author becomes an author (a) because he is vain, (b) because he has an outsize sense of independence and (c) because he hankers after filthy lucre. Not a particularly edifying picture. But of course there is more to it than that. An author is born with a virus in the blood for which there is no cure.

Another question. *How* does anybody become an author?

An author is handicapped in comparison with other creative artists. A singer can go to a school and be taught the theory of music and the proper management of the voice. A pianist can go to a music teacher, a painter to an art school, an actor to a college of drama. But there is no school or college for an author, no paid apprenticeship he can serve. He has to tackle his job alone and unaided. In short, he has to learn by bitter experience.

Then again he must accept that success in his chosen field entails constant hard work, because he can have no paid holidays and his crops don't go on growing while he sleeps. I know a number of people who believe that if they had the time they could dash off something far better than what they are reading in a book or listening to on radio or watching on television. They are prepared to admit that without study they couldn't sing like Moira Anderson or Kenneth McKellar; but because they can, in the old phrase, 'write a good letter', they imagine it takes no toil or tears to become an author, merely time and opportunity. It is a delusion. Admittedly, I am moderately slow witted, but it took me as many years to acquire the skill of writing actable dialogue as it took my friend Davie Watson to become a chartered accountant.

An author must have the ability to survive disappointments, a resilience of temperament and a deep-rooted faith. In boxing parlance, he must have the mental physique to absorb punishment.

He spends three months writing a novel. It is his child, born in travail. Hopefully he sends it out into the world, dreaming of its triumph. Again and again it is rejected. Perhaps, by a stroke of incredible luck, it is finally published. Does his punishment stop there? It is only beginning.

A few reviewers are kind. Others take whips and scourge his child, and he has to bear it and go on producing more children. (Incidentally, I wonder how many people realise what an author has to endure in the way of criticism? How would a grocer or a banker or a farmer like to see paragraphs in the national press, obviously written by a rival grocer or banker or farmer, stating baldly that the goods he is trying to sell or the services he is offering are 'ill constructed rubbish unworthy of serious consideration'. If this happened there would be a court case, and rightly so. But the author has no such redress. It is probably the price of his imagined independence.)

But even if he is spared too much anguish on behalf of his child and is able to reconcile himself to the fact that in terms of book sales his three months' labour has earned him a wage of about £10 a week, further disappointments lie in store. A film company is interested. Adrenalin surges through his blood, and the butler and the Rolls Royce loom nearer. Then silence: utter silence. A letter to the film company is either ignored or answered by a printed slip regretting a lack of production interest. Once again the mirage of the butler and the Rolls Royce vanishes beneath the horizon.

But the bitterest disappointment likely to be experienced by any author is when he finally admits to himself that he may never be as good a writer as he wants to be. He knows what he is aiming at. His ambition is to write with such beauty and precision that in a moment he can convey to a reader, a listener or a viewer the mood of a character, the mood of a place, the mood of a piece of action. William Blake puts the ideal of authorship into four lines:

> To see a World in a Grain of Sand,
> And a Heaven in a Wild Flower,
> Hold Infinity in the palm of your hand,
> And Eternity in an hour.

When the author discovers that such an ideal is beyond him —that, in effect, he is not a genius—then he knows the true meaning of the phrase, *lacrimae rerum*.

Forty years ago, however, all those aspects of authorship were unknown to me.

I suppose I always suspected I would become an author, despite the pressures edging me towards the ministry. The virus was working, and perhaps my stammer was only a signpost on the way.

The Padre had a fine, catholic library in the Manse, and instead of doing my school home-work I usually spent the winter week-ends reading—Stevenson, George Borrow, Seton Merriman, John Buchan—consciously studying the techniques of storytelling and sometimes picturing a day when my own name might appear on the cover of a book. I also became a constant customer at the Campbeltown Free Public Library and found endless pleasure in old bound volumes of the *Strand Magazine,* some of which contained the original Sherlock Holmes stories.

When I was about fifteen I became a fan of Neil Munro and discovered that as well as *John Splendid* and *The Lost Pibroch* he had also written *Para Handy* under the name of Hugh Foulis. I wrote to him, asking for his advice on the task of authorship. I still have his letter, and his advice to a young writer was this: 'Study the old Highland Tales told by a winter's fire. Study the flow and rhythms of our language. Study most of all the strange cantrips of the human heart.'

Six years later, in my third year at the University, I had a short story published in *Chambers's Journal,* an Edinburgh monthly magazine no longer in existence. Called *Vain Words* and loosely based on the Padre's election battle with the Duke of Argyll's factor, it was two thousand five hundred words long, and my fee was five guineas. (For a story of the same length today I should hope to be offered a minimum of £50, though, incredibly, some editors still expect a writer to work for two guineas a thousand.) From then on *Chambers's Journal* was bombarded by MacVicar manuscripts, some of which, against all the odds, found acceptance.

While at University, in addition to *Vain Words,* I sold many other articles and stories to a variety of papers and spent time composing them which, according to prosaic friends, might have been devoted more profitably to swotting for Political Economy. I also—dare I confess it?—wrote poetry, or what I imagined to be poetry. Some of it appeared in *G.U.M.,* the Glasgow University Magazine, under the pseudonym 'Aeneas II'. For three short verses about my girl-friend Jean I was paid ten shillings by an English religious journal, whose editor was obviously under the mistaken impression that the individual on whose 'sweet breast' I longed 'at last to rest' was Jesus Christ.

In 1930, shortly after its foundation in Albion Street, Glasgow, the *Scottish Daily Express* ran a short story contest. I won the first prize, a beautiful rug with a Celtic design made by unemployed Stornoway fisher girls. It still adorns a room in Achnamara, slightly worn at the edges but with its original colours warm and bright. This was the beginning of a long association with the *Scottish Daily Express* and its running mate, the *Glasgow Evening Citizen,* which, though I disagree violently with some of the Beaverbrook opinions, remains happy to this day.

The editor of the *Express* in 1930 was A. C. ('Sandy')

Trotter, who, until he vacated the editorial chair thirty years later to become a director of Beaverbrook Newspapers, continued to buy my work and publicise it. In 1959 my son Jock returned from National Service in Cyprus looking for a job as a sports writer. Sandy Trotter gave him his chance at once, and, in the outcome, I think neither he nor Jock has had cause for regret. Jock now works under the present editor, Ian McColl, who has been as helpful to him as Sandy Trotter was to me. No wonder I have a 'soft side' for the *Express*; and this has nothing whatever to do with the fact that it pays freelances like myself by far and away the highest rates of any newspaper or magazine in Scotland. It is always pleasant to discover that human sentiment has a practical side; but it is the sentiment that counts.

After the débâcle of the Divinity Hall I came home to the Manse in Southend, determined to forget the University and concentrate on becoming an author. The Padre and my mother agreed to accept a pound a week for my board and lodging. I bought a typewriter on the instalment system— seventeen guineas, to be paid off at a guinea a month—and began stringing together thousands of words every day.

Some of the Southend folk thought I was having a lazy time at my parents' expense. The idea that writing might be a difficult and even honourable occupation never occurred to them. In their understanding hard work could only be concerned with physical labour. One old lady used to shout at me from her door: 'Away you go and work!' How much this hurt me, at a time when editors were returning stories and articles by the dozen, I kept strictly to myself.

As an amateur spare-time writer at school and University I had been reasonably successful. Now that I was desperately striving to become a professional I was singularly unsuccessful. Nobody appeared to want my stories any more, not even *Chambers's Journal*. Back came the manuscripts in a flood, accompanied by printed slips each indicating coldly that 'the editor regrets', until at last the situation got so bad that my mother used to meet the post—if she could forestall Old Hugh—and hide the rejection envelopes. (I discovered recently that Jenny Lee often did the same with abusive letters to her husband, Aneurin Bevan.)

However, I was able to continue paying my mother a pound a week and keep up the instalments on the typewriter. This I accomplished (a) by selling scores of short paragraphs to the 'Pertinent and Otherwise' column in the old *Glasgow Bulletin,* at anything up to five shillings a time ('Johnny Crum has been signed by lowly placed Celtic. A crumb of comfort?'), and (b) by competing for money prizes at Highland Games during the summer, where as a sprinter and jumper I sometimes picked up as much as three pounds in a day. After sustaining a nasty gash on the calf of my left leg during a hurdle race at Oban—the residual scar is frequently shown to my friends—I became an expert at avoiding the flying spikes of my equally hungry fellow competitors.

In the end, however, it dawned on me that faith in my own destiny required more practical support. A year after coming home I accepted the offer of regular work on the *Campbeltown Courier* at £3 a week.

10

States of Euphoria

On the *Courier* I was assistant editor, roving reporter, office-boy, sticker-on of labels. Sometimes I got up at six in the morning to help the printers when some big contract was in hand, like wedding invitations or an Agricultural Show Catalogue.

I met all kinds of people—people happy when elected Provost or announced the winner of a football pool, people sad when a relative died or a local fishing-boat was lost—and in the end I learnt from them something of what Neil Munro called 'the strange cantrips of the human heart'. By the editor, Alec MacLeod, one of the many fine journalists I have been privileged to know, I was taught three important lessons.

The first concerned the value of writing clearly, of saying exactly what is meant in the simplest words possible. 'It's easy to use flowery language,' Alec used to say, 'not so easy to be straightforward.' He agreed with J. B. Priestley that a writer ought to be able to share his thoughts and impressions with the crowd. 'Shakespeare could do it,' he would say. 'No intellectual snobbery for him.'

The second lesson was that a writer should have integrity. But integrity, whether moral or artistic, is not so easy to achieve, especially by a young and innocent reporter on a country weekly.

One day I was taken to a pub in Campbeltown by three prominent local men. They flattered my ego, gave me a wonderful party and casually remarked at the end that they would consider it a great favour if I didn't report the cases in which two of them had been fined by the Sheriff for motoring offences. Next day I told Alec, adding that I didn't suppose we should be mentioning the cases anyway, since they were so trivial. I still feel hot and guilty when I remember the dressing-down he gave me for that piece of casuistry. The cases were reported, in full.

On another occasion I was presented with a free pass to the first night of a show by a travelling concert party. I was also presented with a free programme at the door of the Templar Hall and ushered with some ceremony to a seat in the front row. At an interval during the concert there was a prize draw based on lucky numbers on the programme, and with a great show of surprise as she drew the ticket the leading soprano declared me the winner. I saw through that one all right and refused to accept the prize of a pound—big money in those days—insisting that somebody who had paid for his seat and his programme should have it.

Here, of course, the temptation was different: to write a bad notice in order to show the company their mistake in trying to bribe a reporter. But in fact the concert was excellent. I resisted the temptation and recommended it highly in the *Courier*. 'You did right,' Alec said, which made up to some extent for the cruel loss of that pound note.

I must confess, however, that in my career as a storyteller I have often side-stepped integrity and succumbed to temptation, betraying my best instincts for the sake of a cheap effect. But when this has happened I have always been sorry.

The third lesson I learnt from Alec was that good writing is five per cent inspiration and ninety-five per cent perspiration. Each week I had to do a minimum of 5000 words for him, with lineage for outside editors on the side. The hardest and most gruelling task I ever faced, not counting certain spasms of field activity during the war, was the reporting for the *Courier* and other papers of an accident which took place in Campbeltown Loch.

One Sunday afternoon in October, 1933, Jean and I were

walking in the high fields above Brunerican when a boy on
a ramshackle bicycle came panting up to us, announcing
that I must go to Campbeltown at once. There had been an
explosion in a submarine; reporters from all the big dailies
were coming by car and plane, and Alec MacLeod, who was
ill in bed, wanted me to be first on the scene. I kissed Jean
goodbye, ran all the way to the Manse and clattered off in
my old Morris.

On reaching the Quay I found a young fisherman who put
me in the picture.

The previous afternoon, the Second Submarine Flotilla
and the destroyer *MacKay*, having completed a gunnery
exercise in the Firth of Clyde, had left Campbeltown for
Invergordon. In the late afternoon one of the submarines,
L26, had run aground on Paterson's Rock, north of Sanda.
Little or no damage appeared to have been done, so her
crew of fifty officers and men had remained on board. At
floodtide on the Sunday morning she had been refloated,
and the flotilla had returned to the Loch. But while her
batteries were being recharged, the battery-room of L26 had
been destroyed by a violent explosion, caused, it now
seemed, by a dangerous gas created by sea-water coming in
contact with acid in the cells. The explosion had occurred
just as the crew were assembling for dinner on the mess-
deck above the battery-room, and men had been hurled in
all directions. Fire had broken out, with poisonous fumes
spreading into the whole forward structure of the submarine.

Now, as I stood there on the Quay, the injured were
being brought ashore by local skiffs and other small boats,
including the *Verbena,* which belonged to Duncan Newlands.

Some of the injured men's features were unrecognisable.
As first-aid was being rendered to one of them, I heard him
mutter: 'No good working with me. I'm through.' But he
lived.

Straw-packed motor-lorries jostled each other on the

Quay, taking the casualties to hospital, and great work was done by the doctors and hospital staffs. Only two men died, though twenty others were seriously injured or gassed.

The dead were Able Seaman Leonard Rhodes of Leicester and Stoker Fred Whitney of London. Three days later they were buried in a common grave, in a quiet corner of the Campbeltown Cemetery known as the 'Strangers' Neuk', where victims of the sea are put to rest. The afternoon was peaceful, the sun warm, with the scent of autumn in the air. As the buglers sounded the Last Post I could hear the gulls mewing down by the shore. It was a haunting moment which made me think of all the sailors who had died forlornly and far from home.

I don't often cry, except sometimes when offered a moment of supreme artistry by a book, a play or a piece of music. But that afternoon I cried. Perhaps one reason was that I felt empty and exhausted. Evening and weekly papers from Aberdeen to Leicester had been phoning for 'copy' and I had obliged them all. I had also been writing thousands of words about the accident for the *Glasgow Herald* —the only one of the big dailies which hadn't sent a man of its own—and, of course, for the *Courier*.

Even after the funeral the demand for 'copy' continued, and that night I worked until past midnight. Then, after seventy-two hours of continuous action without sleep, I called it a day and went to bed.

The last piece I had written was a 500-word description of the funeral for the *Glasgow Herald*. Next day it was printed under big headlines without a word having been altered. If it hadn't been for the memory of the dead and injured men I should have felt happy and proud. Instead I felt guilty.

Throughout my spell with the *Courier,* which lasted until the end of 1933, I lodged again with Mrs Rankin, from whose large circle of interesting friends in Campbeltown I gleaned many a spicy story for the paper.

At this time Archie was at the University and Willie had joined the Anchor Line as an apprentice; while Rona, Kenneth and John had not yet reached the stage of secondary education. Mrs Rankin, therefore, had a vacancy in her hospitable house for a non-MacVicar, and this was filled by a young classics master at the Grammar School whom I had known at the University.

With his shock of rusty red hair, David Lees was—and is —a live wire, owning perhaps the quickest intelligence of anybody I know. It was no surprise to me when he became Rector of the High School, Glasgow, and eventually took over leading organisational roles in the Educational Institute for Scotland.

Forty years ago neither of us had much money to spare for organised entertainment; but David, with his wisecracks, was an entertainment in himself. Many a time, too, the alert mind in that small body helped me to solve in five minutes a newspaper problem that had nagged in my sluggish brain all day.

Towards the end of our stay in Mrs Rankin's, we both found we had saved enough cash to buy second-hand cars for ourselves. Mine was a 1926 bull-nosed Morris, which cost me £7 10s. David's was a sumptuous 1928 Chrysler, which set him back £12. I have no doubt that one or two sedate matrons in Campbeltown and Southend today remember those cars with nostalgia.

I worked on the *Courier* for more than nine hours every day from Monday to Saturday: sometimes for twelve on a Thursday, which was press day. The printers worked even longer, from six in the morning until six at night, with never an extra penny for overtime.

I did overtime on my own account, however, writing a novel by midnight gas. I finished it with a struggle, seventy thousand words of what was meant to be sophisticated blood and thunder, and sent it off to a London agent. Entitled *The Purple Rock,* it was set in Glasgow and Southend, with a fighting padre as the hero. On 28 October 1932

—my twenty-fourth birthday—I received a letter from Patience Ross of A. M. Heath & Co., Ltd., saying that Frank Cowling of Stanley Paul had accepted it and was offering an advance on royalties of £25.

That was a day of glory.

The Padre was astounded but remarked that when he came to think about it the MacVicars had always been good at telling stories. My mother said she had never doubted I would become a famous writer and quietly remembered that on her mother's side a nineteenth-century Cameron had published a book of Gaelic poetry.

Stung by this unexpected body-blow, the Padre instanced the lady in North Uist who had written *Oran Chlann a Phiocair* and capped his vigorous counter-attack by mentioning Sir Walter Scott's friend, Mrs Grant of Laggan, who had written *Letters from the Mountains*, an eighteenth-century classic. 'She,' he said, 'was a MacVicar.'

'But not,' replied my mother, 'a North Uist MacVicar,' and added inconsequently: 'I had a great-uncle who designed bridges for the Czar of Russia.'

Maimie was stridently triumphant about my success, holding me up as an example of zeal and industry to Rona and my sceptical brothers. The following Sunday, which David Lees and I spent as usual at the Manse, she helped my mother to make a huge dumpling—served with cinnamon sauce—as a mark of celebration.

As for myself, I was in such a state of euphoria that I forgot all about my previous despair and self-criticism and was confident I had written a best-seller. Six months after the publication of *The Purple Rock* in May 1933, the euphoria still lingered and I gave up my job on the *Courier*. Back I came to live at the Manse and launched out with redoubled enthusiasm as a full-time, freelance author.

The truth is, I was extremely lucky with that first book. I got my picture and a column review by Edward Shanks in the *Sunday Times*. Compton Mackenzie, bless his knightly heart, gave it a three-column spread in the *Daily Mail*,

and I am sure that this had nothing at all to do with
the fact that on the first page my hero is discovered reading
a book by Compton Mackenzie. On the whole the Scottish
papers were less enthusiastic, though Mrs MacAulay of the
Oban Times, always a keen supporter of Highland enterprise, published a long and encouraging review, while David
Lees did the same in the *Courier.* (David, in fact, appears in
the book, thinly disguised as the hero's friend.)

In addition to all this, Stanley Paul began advertising *The
Purple Rock* as being in its third impression. My fortune
was made, or so I thought. I became smug and vainglorious,
and my family and the people of Southend—who bought
the book in generous quantities—must have thought me
insufferable.

As it turned out, *The Purple Rock* sold no more than two
thousand copies in hard covers. This brought in only £75,
though later on I collected about £30 from a paperback
edition and £15 for serial syndication rights.

It was my second novel, another long-forgotten masterpiece called *Death by the Mistletoe,* which brought me
properly down to earth. There was a good review in *Punch,*
but Dorothy Sayers in the *Sunday Times* said something
like this: 'It opens promisingly with the murder of three
clergymen but from then on becomes unmitigated drivel.'

When I realised that best-sellers were not for me, my
obnoxious pride and self-confidence gave way to an equally
obnoxious humility and self-pity. Ever since, while giving
birth to sixty other books, I have been struggling to achieve
a kind of precarious balance between the two.

As well as writing poetry to Jean, I courted her for ten long
years. Both her parents were dead, and at the time she was
busy keeping house on the farm for her eldest brother. How,
during that period, she suffered my moods of misery and
exaltation, my states of intermittent poverty and wealth, is a
mystery. How, after thirty-five years of marriage, she continues to suffer them, and even to sympathise with them, is

a greater mystery. Though Kipling's *If* was written about 'a Man', it could well apply to Jean as 'a Woman', especially the lines:

> If you can keep your head when all about you
> Are losing theirs and blaming it on you.

And again:

> If you can meet with Triumph and Disaster
> And treat those two impostors just the same.

We were married in St Blaan's Church at Southend on 24 June, 1936. The service was conducted by the Padre—who else?—assisted by a merry-eyed Kenneth MacLeod.

Archie, who had gained an Honours English degree and was teaching in Dunoon Grammar School, took a plane home to be best man. The bridesmaids were Jean's school friend, Margaret MacLean—who later married 'Boskers'—and my sister Rona.

After the service, proceeding in a taxi to the Inn, where the reception was being held, I had my first taste of marital discipline. Eager to kiss my lovely bride, I was smartly fended off with the remark: 'Don't be silly. You'll muss up my veil!' But at the reception everybody else had a swinging time, though at one stage Jean's nephew John, aged 9, and my brother John, aged 8, came to blows over a glass of lemonade and had to be cuffed into silence by the Padre.

At the time I had about £200 in the bank, so with sublime faith I arranged an overdraft and a loan from the County Council (to be paid back over twenty years) and built a bungalow on the Southend shore, half a mile from Dunaverty and a mile and a half from the Manse. It was to this bungalow, which we called Achnamara, 'the place by the sea', that I took Jean after our honeymoon. We are still there. It would take an earthquake or a tidal wave to shift us now.

On 23 April, 1937, our son Jock was born. That it was St George's Day and Shakespeare's birthday didn't mean as much to us as the fact that he came into the world on Columba's lucky Thursday, 'when the tide began to flow'.

For modern young matrons the onset of pregnancy makes little difference to their activities and social life. Brought up in an old-fashioned school, poor Jean was compelled to retire modestly from public view for three months prior to the birth. The slightest physical exertion was frowned upon, and I remember her disappointment when she was told it might be dangerous even to go in the car. Sometimes we ignored the words of wisdom and went for long hikes in the dark.

In addition to all this, the young mother-to-be was forced to listen to old wives' tales of prolonged and agonising childbirth. My mother tried to minimise the dangers but at the same time told a gruesome story of how her own mother, before the birth of each of her seven children, had spent the time preparing not only baby-clothes but also a shroud for herself. The Padre provided no comfort, either. In his Hebridean code it was a woman's destiny to produce children and a man, having initiated the process, couldn't be expected to take any further practical interest. He is horrified by the idea that a husband might want to be with his wife in the act of childbirth.

When Jock was eventually born it was with difficulty. This is not surprising, in view of his mother's state of unpreparedness, both physical and mental. But Jean soon recovered and settled down to her new task of tending a baby.

Again on old-fashioned advice, she was brainwashed into wrapping him in 'swaddling clothes', i.e., a tight flannel bandage round his middle, which, according to the old wives, would ensure his shapeliness. That the poor infant survived this continuous and uncomfortable physical restriction must have been due to Providence. It appears, however, that in those pre-Spock days the majority of children had to survive it. This majority included Rona, my brothers and myself. 'Look how tall and strong it made you all,' my mother used to say.

Meanwhile, according to Hebridean custom, our son was called after the Padre, his grandfather on the male side, and christened Angus John. Because he was the fifth Angus in succession, and about the twenty-fifth in the line, we began to refer to him as Jock, which prompted a rebuke from an old lady on a neighbouring farm: 'You'd think he was a bull!'

He was christened by his grandfather in St Blaan's, with water taken from St Columba's Well at Kiel. We knew what to expect. When the Padre christens a child there is no gentle dab and finger-tip sign of the cross: he does it thoroughly. That Sunday, reciting the magic words over the baby in my arms, 'I baptise thee, Angus John', he dipped deep into the silver bowl containing the water and sloshed a handful straight into his grandson's face. For a second or two there was silence while Jock gasped and I felt the cold moisture seeping through my right sleeve. Then the church was filled by a series of yells which threatened to shatter the Duchess's stained-glass windows. By my side Jean grew pale but continued staring stoically into space. The choir girls had fits of the giggles. Only some lusty singing of the twenty-third psalm by the crowded congregation brought relief at last.

From 1936 to 1939 life was happy at Achnamara.

The books were selling moderately well. Sandy Trotter had bought one of them, *The Screaming Gull,* for serialisation in the *Express* and was now commissioning regular articles. Willie Ballantine, editor of the *Glasgow Weekly Herald,* William Heddle, editor of the *Bulletin,* and the Rev. J. W. Stevenson, editor then of the *Scots Observer* and later of *Life and Work,* were also buying stories and various features. (Those gentlemen may now have forgotten their kindness to a young and anxious writer, but I haven't.)

Besides all this, I had made contact with the BBC, and in the summer of 1938 my first radio programme was broad-

E

cast, with Alan Melville and James McKechnie in the speaking parts. (What a cast!) It was a documentary for Children's Hour on the subject of herring fishing at Carradale, Kintyre, produced on a shoestring; but I have no doubt that in those days Alan and James were as glad of the meagre money as I was.

In our first three years at Achnamara my annual income from various literary sources was roughly £350—which I reckon is equivalent to about £1500 today—and in spite of a chronic trickle of rejection slips the future seemed rosy enough for Jean, Jock and myself. We had health and independence, sunshine and fresh air, the golf and the beach, and, best of all, the companionship of relatives and good neighbours. Then the war came and spoilt it all.

During the next six years Jean and Jock and I were seldom together. I was forced to give up my pleasant roles as husband, father and slowly succeeding author and become a soldier instead. When and if the war ended, and I survived, I knew with sickening certainty that I should have to begin making my way as an author all over again.

II

His First Command

WHEN the war began in September 1939, Archie was teaching in Dunoon Grammar School, Willie was a fourth mate with the Anchor Line, Rona was at Edinburgh University finishing an Arts degree, Kenneth was also at Edinburgh University in first-year medicine, while John had just gone to the Grammar School in Campbeltown. At Achnamara I was sickening for a mysterious disease.

What the next six years must have cost those of our relatives who stayed at home, waiting and worrying, scarcely bears thinking about.

As a merchant seaman Willie was in the thick of battle from the beginning. Archie joined the Argylls in 1940 and became an officer with the 7/10th Battalion. After graduating, Rona found a teaching post in Campbeltown and was thus able to live with the Padre, my mother and Maimie and help them to take the strain. In 1941, when he was old enough, Kenneth gave up his medical studies, volunteered for the RAF and eventually became a Squadron Leader. (Astonishingly, a hammer toe disqualified him from service with his first love, the Fleet Air Arm.) John continued to attend the Grammar School, which, its buildings commandeered for an ASDIC Training School, was now conducted in cold and dusty halls scattered throughout the burgh.

In December, 1939, Jean was told that I might have galloping consumption. For about four months previously I had been off colour and almost every night shivered with a temperature. The doctors were puzzled. I lost three stones in weight and by Christmas was so weak that I had to stay in bed. The evening temperatures soared higher.

At last tuberculosis was tentatively diagnosed and I was flown by BEA's recently inaugurated Air Ambulance Service to a private nursing home in Glasgow. (The bill for all this was paid for by our friend and neighbour, Mrs Winifred Parsons of Carskiey House, a member of the Coats family of Paisley.)

I remained in St Mary's for eleven weeks, during the first four of which I was at 'death's door', under the care of a chest specialist, a cheerful gentleman with the powerful build and ruddy face of a farmer.

His first act on my being admitted was to fling open the window of my room and issue an order that it must not be closed again until I left the nursing home, cured. In fact, the order was never disobeyed, even when snow fell in early February and an icy wind blew in across my bed. His second act was to announce that my chest was perfectly sound and that whatever might be wrong with me it wasn't consumption.

He asked many questions and discovered that in the previous August, on board Willie's ship, I had eaten a salad prepared by a lascar steward with peculiar toilet habits. Finally, in consultation with his son, who was also a doctor, he diagnosed an Eastern disease, the name and nature of which he never divulged, and began treating me with pills containing arsenic.

The treatment worked. It worked so well that the nightly temperatures were at last reduced to normal. My appetite came back, and I spent all day thinking about my next meal. The only trouble was, when I tried to get out of bed I found my muscles so uncontrollable that I collapsed in a heap on the floor, unable to move.

Nevertheless, it seemed I was now going to live. I put on weight. Arsenic expelled from my system began to powder my hair and whiten my finger-nails. In the middle of March I was back at Achnamara, weak and still stumbling but with a future again.

The memory of one night in St Mary's will always come back to me. I was feverish and unhappy, acutely aware of bodily discomfort. The specialist had just begun administering the arsenic pills, but on this occasion he gave me a shot of something else. (I think it was a tiny dose of morphia, though he always refused to confirm my guess.) Then two of the nurses brought in a friend of theirs who was a singer, and she sang Gaelic songs, there in the room, ending with 'The Lord's my shepherd' to the tune of Crimond. I fell asleep listening to her gentle voice, and this, apparently, was a turning point, because the next day I began to feel better.

The specialist with the appropriate medicine, the nurses with their imaginative care, the singer with a psalm: I was lucky to have had their company in the dark valley.

At many a social gathering my 'illness' had been a pleasurable source of conversation, for me if not for my friends. Not long ago I spoke to a doctor who was genuinely interested in a recital of my symptoms. When I had finished—at long last—he said: 'You know, from what you tell me, I'm almost certain you had brucellosis.'

He may be right. Thirty years ago little was understood about this disease, otherwise known as undulent fever, which is the cause of abortion in cows and can be transmitted through unpasteurised milk to human beings. Only recently has the Government instituted a programme of eradication, which, within a few years, ought to make it as uncommon as bovine tuberculosis.

I volunteered for the Army in October, 1940, and was posted for recruit training to the Argylls at Stirling Castle. My intake was set an intelligence test. When the results were conveyed to us, unofficially, by a sergeant, the recruit with the highest IQ proved to be a young man from Argyll, tall, good looking and with a Charles Atlas physique. He had just been released after a second term in jail for robbery with violence.

Three months later I went for specialist training in bren-gun carriers to Tillicoultry, where one night, on sentry-duty outside the mills in which we were billeted, I heard a distant rumbling and saw in the western sky a firework display of bursting shells, tracer bullets and flaming onions as the Germans bombed Clydebank. I nearly jumped out of my skin, too, when one of the raiders, damaged and limping back to Germany, jettisoned bombs in the glen behind the town.

It was during my spell at Tillicoultry that Willie went missing for twenty-three days. His story is one of many unsung epics of the war.

In the middle of March 1941, under charter from the Anchor Line to the Ministry of War Transport, the 9000-ton liner *Britannia* sailed from Liverpool for India with about 500 passengers and crew, both European and Asian, and a cargo consisting of 9000 tons of war material. At first she was a unit in a convoy, but this split up near the Azores and at dawn on 25 March she was alone, steaming at fifteen knots off the west coast of Africa, in a position approximately 10°38′N, 25°08′W. My brother Willie, the third mate, was among the officers on the bridge.

At 0645 hours a ship was sighted on a south-westerly course, a grey shadow low on the horizon. As the sun came up she began to move in. The Captain became suspicious and altered course, but the strange vessel followed, like a cat.

At 0755 the Captain altered course again, his intention being to steam away, but at this moment the raider opened fire with two-gun salvos. The *Britannia* made smoke and tried to retaliate with her only armament, a four-inch gun mounted on the poop. After firing only twelve rounds, however, a near-miss put it out of action. It had not got the range of the target.

A distress message had been transmitted by W/T as soon as the raider opened fire, but the main aerial had been damaged by one of the early salvos and now *Britannia* was without a voice.

At 0830 the raider was still on the starboard quarter. A smoke float was dropped and *Britannia* altered course slightly to get behind the smoke. This and the funnel smoke gave effective cover, and for a time firing stopped.

Twenty minutes later the smoke lifted and from the bridge Willie saw the German surface raider quite near, a motorship of about 10,000 tons, painted dark grey, with a single large unraked funnel and a Japanese name on the stern. She had four six-inch guns. *Britannia* was defenceless, like a rabbit cornered by a stoat.

At 0915 the raider steamed close and secured a direct hit on *Britannia*'s well-deck. This started a fire. More shells struck *Britannia* amidships, and at 0920 the Captain gave the order to abandon ship. The engines were stopped and steam blown off. Willie went to his post in No. 7 life-boat.

While the life-boats were being lowered and while rafts and pieces of timber were being thrown into the water for stragglers, the raider steamed round to the port beam. At last, when the boats were clear, she fired five salvos at close range, smashing up the forward holds. *Britannia* rapidly filled and sank.

The raider then turned away, dropped a smoke float and steamed off at high speed in a north-westerly direction.

Twenty-seven hours later survivors were picked up by a Spanish freighter and eventually put ashore at Freetown and Gibraltar. All life-boats were accounted for except one. No. 7 was missing.

The life-boat was of a standard type, clinker-built like a whaler, 28 feet long, with a 10-foot beam and a depth of 3 feet 9 inches. She was not equipped with radio.

Along either side a series of large copper buoyancy tanks were covered by longitudinal thwarts. Panels covered the tanks on the inner sides so that they were completely encased. Forward and aft there were small platforms.

Beneath two of the ordinary cross-thwarts were bread tanks. In between were other thwarts at a lower level, under one of which was a fresh water tank and two water breakers.

The mast was twenty feet high, stepped near the foremost thwart. The rig was that of a dipping lug cutter, two sails, fore and main, with only two stays.

This was Willie's first command. All he said about her afterwards was that he found her 'damned difficult to sail'. He ought to know. With 81 other men, 17 European and 64 Asian, she was his little world for the next twenty-three days. Her official complement was 56.

The other boats had vanished in the confusion of smoke when the *Britannia* sank and the raider steamed away. Now, making water fast, necessitating vigorous bailing, Life-boat No. 7 ran before the wind on a southerly course. At sundown Willie issued one bottle of water to be shared by everybody.

All night the fit men baled hard. One Asian refused to help, saying he had paid for his passage in *Britannia*. Willie explained that the situation had changed: they were now, in more senses than one, all in the same boat. The man saw the point.

In the morning they hoped they might still be picked up. At the same time they had to face the possibility of a long voyage. After conferring with a number of naval officers in the boat, Willie made up his mind. The obvious thing was to sail for the coast of Africa 600 miles away; but the wind was against them, and he decided, therefore, to try for Brazil, which meant a journey of 1200 miles. They set course west-south-west and ran before a fresh wind. (A fortnight later, in the Manse, Old Hugh was comforting my mother with his firm conviction that this was what Willie must have done.)

The boat was leaking badly, and shrapnel holes were discovered below the water-line. These were plugged and covered with tingles made from a tobacco-box. At seven o'clock in the evening a ship was sighted eight miles away, but she failed to see them.

Willie then initiated a sorting out process. Those on

board were divided into groups, Asian crew members in the bows, Asian passengers amidships, Europeans in the stern. An inventory was made of the contents of the boat. The water breakers, containing sixteen gallons between them, were moved aft for safety. It was confirmed that the only food on board consisted of two bins of ship's biscuits and forty-eight cans of condensed milk. A ration order was laid down. At sunrise each man would get one biscuit spread with condensed milk and at sundown a biscuit and a third of a dipper of water (about an eggcupful).

On the second day most men discarded their life-belts. At noon another ship was sighted in the distance, but she also failed to see them. A few of the Asians were spotted drinking sea-water and warned. In the afternoon the wind died away and poor progress was made.

Early in the morning of the third day, 28 March, they saw the steaming lights of yet another ship. They fired flares and burned some of their clothes but without result. As the wind freshened the main halyards broke and had to be repaired.

Most of the Asians were now helping to bale, thanks to the authority of an enormously fat Indian merchant, who had promised Willie he would get the others to work if he himself were allowed to concentrate on a course of prayer. A rota of duties was arranged for the Europeans.

On 29 March the strain began to tell and several men fainted. Willie and his companions cleaned their section of the boat and tried to wash, stripping to the waist and lying over the gunwale while others poured sea-water over them from tins. Fishing hooks and spinners were improvised when a shoal of fish came alongside, but nothing was caught.

That night many had their first sleep since leaving *Britannia*. Next day at noon, with clearer head, Willi estimated that they had covered 300 miles. He altered course to the south-west. They saw several 'Portuguese Man-of-War' fish. One of the naval officers fixed up a sea anchor ready for immediate use. At sundown many complained that they found their biscuit difficult to swallow owing to thirst. It was a Sunday, so they sang *Abide with Me* and Willie said the Lord's Prayer, the only prayer he knew.

Afterwards, as darkness fell, thoughts elbowed each other in his mind. They formed a pattern which, though differing in detail and clarity, recurred time after time in the succeeding days.

. . . Sooner or later a ship is bound to see us. Surely, surely, surely. So far we have just been unlucky. I hope nobody has guessed how worried I am.

It's queer. Before we get to South America we must cross the Equator, and in all my eleven years at sea I have never crossed the Equator. If I survive, it will be something to boast about that the first time I crossed the Line was under sail.

My first command, and this is it—a twenty-eight-foot lifeboat, leaky and overloaded, limping across the Atlantic. When I was a wee boy I remember climbing a tree in the Manse garden to watch the Atlantic liners pass the Mull of Kintyre. Even then I meant to be a sailor, and I used to dream about my first command—the Caledonia *or the* Transylvania *or even* Britannia *herself. But in a way this is just as important: eighty-one lives depending on me.*

The heat is getting worse. Exposure, thirst and fear: these are the enemies. Thirst is much worse than hunger. Somewhere I read that to suck a button can help. I have told the others this, and some of us are sucking buttons, but the relief is only marginal. The water lapping against the side of the boat is a temptation. I have a five-cent piece in my pocket. On Pier 54 in New York I could use it to get an ice-cold drink from one of the orange-juice containers.

The glens at home will be cool and green, and at this time of year, under the trees at the Manse, the lilies should be coming out. I can see Nina there, beautiful and fresh in her nurse's uniform. Will I ever see her again? She promised to marry me when I came back. . . .

Next morning a mouthwash was made of condensed milk

and sea-water. It made little difference to their thirst and left a foul-smelling scum on their teeth and gums.

That evening a stout and friendly Goanese cook who had sailed with Willie in several ships accepted his water ration and drained it at a gulp. There was something odd about his eyes. Willie asked him if he had been drinking sea-water, but he only smiled and shook his head. He was lying.

Afterwards he sat quietly enough until about ten o'clock, when he began to chatter to himself, describing meals he would cook for them, talking about the wife and two lovely children in Goa whom he loved so much. At midnight he started to scream. At half past one in the morning he leapt on to the gunwhale, calling out for his wife, and threw himself overboard.

The first death. The first of how many?

The days began to merge into each other. It was impossible to relax. Sleep came only in snatches as emaciated bodies pressed against protuberances of wood and iron. Most of the men were suffering from salt-water boils.

As the boat neared the Equator it grew hotter. Tongues were swollen, lips cracked. Men grew silent and still, and then died. A few crawled away and jammed themselves into small spaces behind the buoyancy tanks, out of which their stiffened bodies could be prised later only with difficulty.

The dead were lifted over the side and dropped into the sea. Some sank at once. In calm weather others floated beside the boat for a long time, like sodden bundles of washing. Willie says that in time he began to feel 'immune from death'. This loss of sensitivity worried him.

One night the Asians in the bow started quarrelling amongst themselves. Willie crawled forward and found a man with a knife, its blade flashing in the moonlight. Cold and shivering with fear, he asked the man to give it up. The man did so and began to cry.

On the fifteenth day, 8 April, black storm clouds gathered, and it rained hard for several hours. A few gallons of rain water were collected in a sail. That night, at sundown,

Willie dispensed what he called a 'milkshake', a cupful of water mixed with condensed milk. Some of the men put their biscuits in a cloth or handkerchief and soaked them in water, but this made them only a little easier to swallow and not at all more palatable.

As it grew dark a violent storm blew up. They had to lower the mainsail and run before the wind, baling frantically.

Everybody was cold and wet after the storm. One of the naval officers went down with malaria, shivering violently. Willie and another naval officer stretched close beside him at night to share the heat of their bodies.

By now the physical state of those in the boat was pitiful. Willie wrote: 'Each of us has lost pounds in weight and the bones of the body are becoming more pronounced. Beneath straggling growths of beard faces are drawn and haggard. The skin is drawn tightly over protruding cheek bones. The ears look abnormally large. The eyes are bloodshot and sunk back into the head. Beards and hair are tufted and matted with salt and sweat. To do anything is becoming more and more of an effort, even turning to try and sit in a more comfortable position. The dazzling light from the sun causes a dull pain behind the eyes, and sometimes vision is blurred.'

Even his dreams were blurred. Nina, the five-cent piece for orange-juice, the lilies at the Manse, all were now the stuff of nightmares. His body was hot, his skin dry, his thirst almost unbearable. When an Indian crew member went berserk through drinking sea-water he fought with him and prevented him from jumping over the side. It did no good. The man died anyway.

A ship was seen on 11 April, and another on 12 April. But both passed on, unaware of Life-boat No. 7.

April 13 was Easter Sunday. The sea was choppy, and during the night good progress had been made in a freshening wind. Some rain water had been collected during the showers, and for breakfast that morning a double ration of the 'milkshake' was handed round. In the past days Willie had learnt how to pray. He now conducted a short service, during which the survivors sang an Easter hymn, followed by 'The Lord's my shepherd'. But before nightfall another man died.

On April 14, their twenty-first day in the boat, they saw a seagull. They stared at it, almost unable to believe. But then they heard its melancholy cry and in a kind of numb amazement realised that land must be near.

Next morning, April 16, excitement was intense. When the breeze came up it brought an earthy smell. The water became 'a dirty shore green' and floating in it they saw the branch of a tree.

Land was sighted at 1140 hours. By 1600 hours they were running north-west along the coast, unable to reach it because of the surf.

During the night they stood well out. At dawn there was no sign of land. In a panic Willie altered course to the south-west and at noon it was again visible.

At 1600 hours they waded and staggered ashore on the island of Corupu, where, with difficulty, they made camp for the night.

The following morning they were found by three native fishermen who cooked for them a meal of *farinha,* a mixture of manioca flour and fish, and gave them shelter in their huts. With his stick one of the fishermen wrote in the sand 'BRASIL'. Willie gave this man a written message, which next day reached the British vice-consul in San Luiz de Maranhao across the channel.

On April 19, twenty-five days after the sinking of the *Britannia,* the scarecrow occupants of Life-boat No. 7 were taken in canoes to San Luiz. Of the original eighty-two only thirty-nine survived.

That same afternoon a telegram was delivered at the Manse in Southend. In triumph Old Hugh said to my mother, 'I kent fine he'd be a' richt!'

During the voyage Willie reckons he lost one and a half

pounds every day. He had a suppurating wound in his foot, but this was quickly cured in the San Luiz General Hospital, and he felt no further ill effects. All the other Europeans, starved of water for so long, suffered for a time with kidney trouble. Willie's kidneys were pronounced to be in excellent condition. He omitted to tell the doctor that for six weeks, at the age of four, he had been seriously ill at the Manse with Bright's disease.

Not long afterwards, 'as a result of suggestions put forward by officers and men of the Merchant Navy who have suffered trying ordeals during long voyages in open boats', the Minister of War Transport told Parliament that many new safety regulations were being introduced for ships' lifeboats. They would be equipped, for example, with radio sets that could send out automatic distress signals. They would carry larger quantities of food and water, and more varied kinds of food. Hand pumps would be fitted, and each life-boat would be supplied with oil for massaging feet and legs.

Willie got an MBE for his trouble. Unfortunately, when they went to London for the Investiture, he and Nina, now safely married, forgot to pack his uniform trousers and only a last-minute rush by the Army and Navy Stores saved the day.

12

Beyond the Chindwin

IN 1942 Archie went overseas with the Argylls. He took part in the Battle of El Alamein. In the advance which followed he was wounded and later mentioned in despatches. His friends tell me that he won this 'mention' in the action for which his commanding officer was awarded the Victoria Cross.

In 1943 he was in Sicily. During the battle for Catania in July, his battalion was on the left of mine, the 2nd Royal Scots Fusiliers. When the immediate fighting ended I took a jeep and in some excitement went across to see him. I was just too late. The driver of an Argylls truck told me he had been killed at Gerbini the day before.

I went to see his temporary grave. One of my sergeants took a photograph of me standing near the white stones which surrounded it. This I sent home to the Manse. It was all I could do.

One night my mother dreamt that she saw me standing beside a grave surrounded by white stones. At breakfast next morning she mentioned this to the Padre, and the same day the telegram announcing Archie's death arrived from the War Office. My photograph came a fortnight after that.

The Padre firmly believes that my mother had the second sight.

Archie was the honest one, the handsome one. Before joining the Army he married Mima Greenshields, another young teacher in Dunoon. Their happy life together was short.

Mima suffered the blow of her husband's death with

courage and dignity and made up her mind to visit the military cemetery at Catania to which his body had been moved. Other considerations, too, were dulling the pain of her personal tragedy. 'I knew so little of how it happened. I felt it important that somebody should be there with the wounded, to try to take the place of their relatives.'

But how to accomplish these urgent aims? It seemed to her that the only answer was to resign as a teacher, join the Red Cross and apply for a posting to the Mediterranean; and because in her own quiet way Mima can move mountains, she was in the Red Cross and in Sicily within a few weeks.

She saw where Archie is buried. As a welfare officer she talked to wounded men in hospital and concerned herself with their comfort. If they died she wrote to their friends at home, the most difficult task of all.

I met her in Italy in 1944, thanks to a romantic Italian engine-driver who stopped our troop train at a place where I knew she'd be waiting. There were wolf whistles from my Fusiliers as I stepped out and met a glamorous-looking Mima on the platform and kissed her. They had no idea she was my sister-in-law, and neither had the engine driver. Smiling from ear to ear, he spent more than half an hour taking on water, an operation scheduled to last only five minutes.

When the war ended Mima remained with the Red Cross. In 1946 she was appointed Senior Welfare Officer in Greece, where she acted as liaison officer between the British Army and the Greek Red Cross in the rehabilitation of Greek hospital patients, whose need of medicine and clothing was desperately urgent. 'There were scores of children quite capable of being out and about,' she says, 'who had to remain in hospital because they didn't have any clothes.' In recognition of her pioneer work in this field Mima left Greece with a diploma and the first honorary membership badge of the Greek Red Cross Society. She left it, too, with an abiding affection for the people of Greece.

Then began her years with the Overseas Department of

the British Red Cross, during which she helped with the development of no less than fifteen branches and with the establishment of four independent national societies in Malaya, Nigeria, Uganda and Guiana.

She remembers with pride the formation of the Nigerian society. In his speech, the white president of the former branch suggested the appointment of a distinguished coloured man as president of the new national body. Whereupon the coloured man, shaking his head and smiling, pointed out that the Red Cross makes no distinctions in regard to race or colour. 'I should be honoured to serve as vice-president,' he said, 'but my white colleague, with all his experience, is the best new president we could possibly get. Why should he step down just because he is white?'

Annually, Mima travelled thousands of miles, arguing, persuading, achieving miracles of co-operation. In fact, nobody argues with her for long. Behind her charm there is a steely dedication, both spiritual and physical, that never wavers.

She knows more about violence and its aftermath than any soldier or soap-box politician. If she could be persuaded to write her story it would make a James Bond thriller appear pale in comparison. Unfortunately, getting Mima to talk about her adventures is like trying to open a can of fruit with a safety-pin.

In Malaya, when terrorism was at its height, she set up local Red Cross branches all over the country, a first step in the formation of a national society. To begin with, she and her team were given military and police protection; but after experiencing several ambushes ('You didn't have time to think about catching a stray bullet, you just ducked!') Mima decided it was safer for Red Cross workers to travel unescorted. This proved to be the case, because even the bandits had respect for the Red Cross.

After the fall of Tshombe in the Congo, she risked her life to bring aid to the refugees. She organised one convoy of food and clothing in Zambia and led it across the border, sometimes dining off rice and canned milk taken from

ditched trucks. She faced trigger-happy Congolese gen-
darmes demanding petrol on a lonely road and left them
muttering and baffled, still without petrol. 'I was scared.
Sure. But I knew I was expendable.'

In Cyprus once, during the Eoka troubles, when British
servicemen never left camp except in convoys bristling with
guns, she drove alone and unarmed through the guerilla
country to visit her nephew—my son Jock—who was
soldiering there with the Argylls. 'I have unshaken faith in
this,' she often says, pointing to her Red Cross badge. 'I
believe the safest person in the world is a lone woman wearing it.'

On her recent retirement from the Red Cross, after nearly
a quarter of a century in its service, she was given its highest
award—only twenty-five people can hold it at one time—
the Certificate of Honour and Badge, Class I. Like Willie,
she also received an MBE for her trouble.

Mima is tall and elegant, with an air of detachment. This
detachment is not only the mark of a lifetime of unselfish
work but also her armour against emotional involvement in
cases of suffering all over the world. But, being a woman,
she admits that her armour has a few chinks. One appeared
in a depressing Italian hospital, when a grievously wounded
eighteen-year-old gunner clung to her, begging her not to
leave him. Another showed in Antigua when she visited the
leper colony, 'the kind of place where rats came out at night
to gnaw the patients.' Her detachment, however, can un-
expectedly vanish behind laughter at a family joke or
enthusiastic gossip concerning her numerous nephews and
nieces.

She remains extremely busy, looking after her widowed
brother's young family. The babies, she says, are much more
dangerous than Grivas's cut-throats.

She has never had much money to spend; but the riches
she has given away in service to others is beyond the reckon-
ing of a millionaire.

Archie must be proud of her.

In December 1944, Mima was still in Italy. Kenneth, then only twenty-three, was stationed on the central Burma Front, in charge of B Flight, 28 Squadron, flying Hurricanes from the airstrip at Tamu in the valley of Imphal. The squadron's major task was to carry out close reconnaissance for forward Army units. A minor one was to beat up the Japs whenever they were seen, which wasn't often. At last the Far East war was going well, with the enemy in retreat.

On 22 December, early in the morning of a sunny day, Kenneth climbed aboard Hurricane 299. He checked his kit: the 'blood money' belt containing rupees; the pistol belt with a kukri added to it; the parachute with its escape harness attached to the seat; the needle compass in the lapel of his green battledress. He checked also that there was nothing in his pockets except a handkerchief.

He took off down the bumpy mud strip, trying as always not to dwell on the fact that he was going to spend the next few hours seeking the destruction of men he had never seen, while at the same time they would be doing their best to kill him. Wheels up over the trees and he was on his way.

He crossed the Chindwin just north of Mawlaik and was soon over the jungle proper. Then he saw the road, the road down which the advance of the Fourteenth Army would come.

The Jap himself was invisible, but small details betrayed his whereabouts: the larger than usual concentrations of cattle, heavy layers of dust on roadside trees, jumpy Burmese scurrying away at the sound of an aircraft. Kenneth made little memos on his knee pad and made notes of map references. He swept over a place called Yeu and spotted a Jap attending to the wants of nature, literally with his trousers down. Standing the Hurricane on its ear, he came round fast and 'knocked spots off the place' with his four twenty-millimetre cannon.

Suddenly, on the way home, over Kinbin, he noticed tracer coming up at him. This was what he had been looking for, a definite response from the enemy. He swung away, turned and came weaving down on the machine-gunner. What happened next is best told in his own words.

'When strafing like this, you have to remember you are most vulnerable when pulling away from the target. The gen is to keep low on the exit and weave about like mad. This I did, but too well. In my line of flight was a tree taller than the rest. I pulled the Hurricane up with all my strength, but too late. The machine bounced off the top of the tree but strangely kept on flying. Then I noticed the temperature gauge: it was going off the clock. The radiator had been damaged and the engine was about to go on fire.

'There was no question of baling out; I had to try to land. I saw an open space with some paddy fields whose bunds didn't look too steep. It would have to be there. I came in, put the Hurricane down rather too early, bounced from one field into the other. The dirt flew: if I'd hit the next bund it would have been curtains. But suddenly the machine slewed round and there was silence.

'First came relief that I was down and uninjured, then the terrible knowledge that I had landed some fifty miles behind the enemy lines, an enemy in retreat and reported to be at his most vicious. Loosening the harness, I jumped out and ran as fast as I could to the nearest clump of trees.'

On his own admission he was terrified, but at this point discipline and training took over from conscious thought. The first rule was to bury his parachute. He did so. The second rule was to destroy the aircraft. But there was nothing of any value in it. Would anyone blame him for not going back to it, with the risk of being seen? He found his legs carrying him down through the paddy field; he found his fingers taking off the safety-cap of the little 'emergency bomb', striking it on the nose of the propellor and throwing it into the cockpit. Duty done, he 'retreated smartly' to his hideout.

In a minute or two he was joined in the thicket by a Burmese who had obviously seen him crash. Something about this man was 'different'. Kenneth took out his sheet of

Burmese phrases: 'I am a British airman. If you help me escape I will give you money. Can you get me water?' All the stranger could do was giggle, and Kenneth realised what was different about him: he was insane. As the man ran off, suddenly shouting with laughter, Kenneth's skin turned cold. This was a terrible portent. For a moment his Hebridean ancestry took over, and he wanted to cry with self-pity.

But at last he pulled himself together and crept out of his hide. Running from cover to cover he started off in a northerly direction.

Everything was quiet. There were a few cattle about but no people. He came to a clearing and with surprise saw an old woman sitting on a paddy bund. She was placidly smoking a green cigar and looked a solid type, so he decided to make her acquaintance. Her calmness was good for him: it settled his nerves.

But seeing her smoke made him desperate to do the same. He started to struggle with his airtight escape-kit box, trying to get it open. The old lady watched him dispassionately, then with a smile pointed to his kukri. With this he managed to prize the box open sufficiently to take out a tin of cigarettes and a packet of barley sugar. He offered his new acquaintance some of the barley sugar but she refused.

He took out his phrase-sheet again: 'Are there many Japanese near here?'

'Too many,' she told him, pointing, and at the edge of the forest he saw a long stream of people. 'Run,' she said.

Kenneth writes: 'I didn't wait for a second bidding. Picking up my escape box I ran, crouching low, until I was among the trees. I stopped and looked back. She was still sitting there, unmoved. She had seen it all before, but I felt her heart had been with the fugitive.'

He now gave reasoned thought to his situation and decided that since there was no chance of him being picked up from the air he must try to walk the fifty miles back to Imphal through the Japanese lines.

Later in the day, peering out from deep undergrowth, he saw men, women and children working in a field beside a village. They seemed to be a settled community, and there was no sign of any Japanese. He attracted the attention of one of the younger men and asked him in Burmese if he could help. Eventually another youth agreed to show Kenneth the path to the north as far as the main road if in return he got fifty rupees. Kenneth accepted the bargain; but after leading the way for about two miles the youth suddenly stopped and refused to go on. He held out his hand for the reward. Sick at heart Kenneth gave him five rupees.

Plodding on alone, Kenneth reached a little knoll in a clearing. As he lay there, resting, a Hurricane passed over, then another, weaving about at low level and evidently looking for him. He got out the metal mirror which was part of his escape kit and flashed it in the sun to attract their attention. They failed to see it.

He sucked a Horlicks tablet from the escape box and smoked a cigarette. As he prepared to move on again he heard voices approaching along the path and saw to his astonishment the youth who had deserted him a few hours earlier, along with another Burmese older and stronger. Revolver in hand, he went to meet them.

There was a chaos of explanation. The youth had gone back to find this older man, who, it seemed, knew the country well. Together they would take Kenneth back to the British lines for the remaining forty-five rupees.

Kenneth was becoming wary of large promises but decided to accept the offer. Before they set off, the big Burmese started digging in the sand. When he had gone down about a foot the hole began to fill with water. Cupping his hands, he drank from it and motioned Kenneth to do the same. It was a valuable lesson in the art of living rough.

That night they reached a village which his companions declared was free of Japanese, but as they rounded a bend fifty yards away Kenneth saw a Japanese soldier. walking towards them, obviously on sentry duty. He fled, the Burmese following more slowly at his heels. 'Wrong village,' the older man said, somewhat unnecessarily.

Two miles further on they came to another village. This one did appear to be safe. But at first the headman was quite adamant. He could not risk hiding a British airman while the Japanese were in the vicinity.

Then Kenneth remembered something the instructor in his Escape Class had told him: 'If you get on the right side of the children, the Burmese will do anything you want.' He took out a handful of barley sugar and handed it round. The children sucked and drooled with pleasure, and the attitude of the headman and the other villagers began to thaw. Finally the headman promised to hide him and sent a young girl to fetch him something to eat.

As he sat on the verandah of the headman's house, now almost completely exhausted, there was a sudden commotion in the village. Into the square ran the young girl who had been sent for food, screaming with fear. Behind her, rifles at the ready, came a platoon of helmeted Japanese soldiers. This was it, then. Kenneth stood up and put his hands above his head.

The first bullet went singing past his left ear, the second somewhere between his legs. He didn't wait for any more. Obviously they had no intention of taking him prisoner, so he might as well die running. But where to?

Fortunately the village was like a maze. As he dodged and ducked he was pursued by shots and shouting people. Round the entire village was a thick hedge. He dived into it, but on the other side he saw open ground which would make him an easy target if he tried to cross it.

Though breathless and desperately frightened, Kenneth dredged up some native cunning. He doubled back and went to ground in a large thicket inside the village. But soon a Japanese NCO approached the thicket and began to probe into it with the bayonet on his rifle. Systematically he worked his way round until he was opposite Kenneth's hiding-place. He plunged the bayonet in and missed him by about six inches.

Then the darkness came down with merciful swiftness. The noise and the shouting died away.

Some hours later Kenneth reached a dried-up river-bed and on the other side lay down in a patch of long, dry grass and pulled it over him. A miracle happened. He fell asleep. He didn't wake up until it was daylight. As he stood up he heard a cock crowing in the distance.

He began to walk along a path which followed the *wadi* he had crossed during the night. There was good cover, and he got the impression that the whole country was deserted. 'Suddenly,' he writes, 'there was a whistle behind me. Coming along the path were the two Burmese who had been with me the previous day. They had plates of food, rice and some green stuff which didn't look at all appetising. I was so hungry, however, that at once I took some of the rice in my hands. As I did so I detected movement in the high grass near the river-bed. Sure enough there were the Japanese soldiers again. Had they been brought by the Burmese? I flung the rice from me and raced off again, seeking refuge among the trees.'

After his varied experience of Burmese hospitality he decided from then on he would go it alone and speak to no one. He had lost all his escape kit and had nothing left except his money belt, his revolver with one bullet in it and his compass. But he had a reasonable knowledge of the terrain and reckoned that if he travelled two days due north he could then turn west and come to the Chindwin, well inside the British lines.

All that day he trudged through the forest, sometimes speaking to himself and resting for long periods whenever he thought he heard movement. He had a continuous thirst, but he always found water in the sand, digging for it in the way his questionable Burmese friend had done. Then, having drunk his fill, he would wonder what dread diseases he might have picked up in the brackish water.

When darkness came he slept fitfully. The moon rose and he made up his mind to try travelling by night; but after falling once or twice on the uneven ground he was forced to wait until daylight. Moonlight is rarely as bright as one imagines.

The third day was uneventful, though just as dangerous, because he began to experience attacks of lethargy. This, he supposed, was a result of hunger. He climbed some trees to pick coloured berries, but they all proved to be hard and wooden. He came to a shallow river and cooled his burning face in it.

The following day was Christmas. When he awoke from a sleep disturbed by thoughts of *Silent Night* being sung in the church at Southend, he could hear voices. Taking the revolver from its holster, he crept towards the sound and among the trees saw a ragged group of Burmese. At one end of their encampment a pot was boiling on a fire of twigs.

When he emerged from the forest they cringed away. They explained they were hiding in the jungle until the war was over. Food was their main problem, and they were only just managing to exist. The pot on the fire contained some sweet potatoes, all the food available for the group.

Kenneth told them rather desperately that he hadn't eaten for three days, and with reluctance the headman lifted the lid and took out four small potatoes. Kenneth ate one. It had little or no taste and, strangely, he didn't feel like eating the rest. He put them in his pocket and left the sad gathering among the trees. 'I had to survive too,' he says.

Now he was travelling west against the run of the land, which meant climbing up steep slopes and sliding down into ravines on the other side. But about mid-day he saw something which made him forget his weariness. A squadron of Dakota planes flew over and started dropping supplies to the south-east. He had made it. British forward units must be in the area. His only problem now was whether to retrace his steps towards the supply drop or go forward

until he met up with other British troops. Unable to face
the thought of going back, he decided to go on.

Late in the afternoon he reached a stream running
between precipitous banks. He slid down to the water and
drank some, and then looked up at the bank on the other
side. It was steep and rough, thick with boulders and undergrowth, but his will drove him on and he began to climb. As
he strained upwards into the last few feet he was almost
utterly exhausted; but he saw a little sapling on the top edge
and caught it. The sapling broke. He tumbled back down
through the boulders into the stream.

For a moment or two he lay dazed. Then, once again, his
training took over. He remembered his instructor's voice:
'If you are on the run, and get a chance, take your boots off
and wash your feet. You'll feel better afterwards.' So he
roused himself, took off the marching boots he had now
been wearing for four days, peeled off the socks that were
almost vulcanised to his flesh and put his feet into the water.

His strength did indeed come back a little, but he felt unable to face the steep bank a second time. From then on he
would have to follow the run of the country, which was
south-west. He put on his socks and boots, therefore, and
began walking downstream.

Occasional machine-gun fire rattled fairly close, and he
was confident that sooner or later he would find some
British troops. Towards nightfall he heard voices and saw,
coming along the riverside, a group of soldiers. Elated, he
started to run towards them. Then he noticed their helmets.
They were Japanese.

He dived into the undergrowth, feeling sick and sorry for
himself. It looked as if after all he wasn't going to make it.
The only saving grace was that the Japs hadn't seen him
yet.

He writes: 'I had no time to think of what to do next,
because I found myself suddenly in the midst of a hellish
noise. The whole earth shook; bits of trees flew around.
Heavier pieces of something splashed into the river-bed, at

this point almost dry, throwing up plumes of sand. It came
to me that this was an artillery barrage, and from its inten-
sity I was sure it was being laid down by the Fourteenth
Army. Was I going to be killed by British guns?'

At the approach of darkness the shelling stopped. On
every side he could hear a great many Japanese moving
about and talking amongst themselves, obviously unhappy
with their situation. He lay in the bush only a few yards
away, under no illusions as to what would happen if they
found him. He didn't sleep, afraid he might cry out in a
troubled dream. In the troubled reality he didn't move a
muscle.

When daylight came the area grew quiet. Once or twice
he thought he heard voices but couldn't be sure if they
belonged to friend or foe. Lying motionless in the heat of the
bush, he began to lose control of himself. Momentarily he
would drop off to sleep and experience the wildest hallucina-
tions. He dug his nails into his palms, willing himself to
stay awake and still.

Again darkness came, and he was relieved to notice that
the Japanese had thinned out. Now there was only an odd
whispered conversation, an odd twig breaking underfoot.
He wondered if the enemy were pulling out. During that
night he slept fitfully, sometimes dreaming that he was home
in Southend, safe in the Manse garden.

Soon after dawn he saw tanks whining up along the river-
bed. Shells from the tanks thudded into the hillside and he
cowered in his hiding-place. They were British tanks, but he
was afraid to show himself in case some Japanese snipers
might have been left behind, or in case the tank commanders
took him for an enemy.

The tanks moved on. About three o'clock in the afternoon
there appeared along the riverside a continuous stream of
jeeps and marching men. When they were about a hundred
and fifty yards away, he took off the white scarf he had been
wearing. Lying behind a tree-trunk he tentatively waved it.

'I've never seen men move more quickly. A whole jeep-load were on their bellies with rifles cocked and pointing in my direction before I could take it in.

'An officer came towards me. I decided to risk it. With my hands above my head I went out to meet him.

'He saw me, dirty, gaunt, unshaven and doubtless wild of eye. His expression was comical. He said: "Who the bloody hell are you?"

'My friends with the rifles decided to take a closer look. When they learned who I was they shook hands with me and with each other. There had been an inter-battalion sweepstake on the chances of my being picked up alive, and they had won it.

'I had fallen into the hands of the Gordon Highlanders. That was good enough for me.'

On demobilisation, Kenneth gave up the idea of medicine. He married his Isabel and began studying for the Church at St Andrews University; and in course of time, to their deep satisfaction, the Padre and my mother got a minister in the family after all.

Kenneth was awarded a DFC and, with Mima and Willie, later joined the MBE club. John and I feel slightly out of it.

John, however, has no reason to bemoan the paucity of letters after his name. At the last count he had twelve, all relevant to his profession as a doctor specialising in obstetrics and gynaecology. He is nineteen years younger than I am—what Gaelic folk call a *troich,* meaning the last, unexpected wee pig in a litter—and his career so far has borne out my theory that the youngest of a family is, as a rule, the brainiest.

He did another clever thing in marrying a Sassenach, a Yorkshire girl called Esmé.

13

The Ironclad Snowdrop

THE war for me was less hazardous than for Archie, Willie
and Kenneth. In five years, as they say, I 'didn't get a
scratch'. Reviewed from a distance of more than a quarter
of a century, my career as a temporary officer and gentleman emerges as a patchwork of vividly remembered inci-
dents, some comic, some tragic, with obscure areas of
boredom in between.

I detest the idea of war, which releases and then tolerates
the primitive lusts, particularly the lust to maim and kill,
and tears down the tentative frail growth of civilised
behaviour. Nevertheless, in retrospect, I enjoyed being a
soldier, perhaps because war poses a curious paradox: the
comradeship of men facing danger together is often finer and
more enduring than the comradeship of men in sheltered
civilian occupations.

My first experience of active service occurred in March,
1942, when we sailed north from Liverpool in a convoy,
shepherded by destroyers and the battleship *Ramillies*. On
the way out through the North Channel, I stood at the rail
at about four o'clock in the morning and saw the dark
shadow of the Mull of Kintyre only a few miles away to
starboard, where Jean and Jock in Achnamara, and the
Padre, my mother, Maimie and John in the Manse, were all
probably asleep.

To begin with, the move was called Operation Snowdrop,
and the rude and licentious soldiery had something to say
about that. My batman, Fusilier McClymont—called 'Jaggy
Feet' on account of his bunions—had a four-letter word

which described exactly what ought to be done with such a misbegotten flower.

But somewhere along the line, as we played hard-to-get with German submarines in the Atlantic, the frustrated little poet in the War Office must have been replaced by a snarling General with an outsize moustache, because after we had spent five weeks in the old P & O liner *Oronsay* and were at last approaching the coast of Africa, we discovered that Operation Snowdrop had become Operation Ironclad. Instead of finding a cushy billet at Trincomalee in Ceylon, we were going to invade Madagascar.

Our PT sessions began to borrow overtones from the Inquisition. I remember in the tropics doing press-ups on the open deck and seeing the sweat dripping from my nose and hearing a tough front-row forward beside me muttering: *'Gentle Jesus, meek and mild ...'*

Then somebody chalked out the diagram of an LCA—a landing-craft, assault—and we tiptoed about the deck like children playing hopscotch, while so-called 'experts' instructed us in the proper method of getting into it. How we were to get out of it, presumably under withering fire from the enemy on the beach, was left to our imaginations.

At that time, almost every other Allied unit in Britain except ourselves had for months been practising assault landings with real LCAs. Why did the High Command choose us to carry out the first full-scale seaborne invasion of enemy territory in World War II? Was it just another example of their genius for tactical surprise? McClymont and I, pretending to be professional soldiers, would have surprised anybody.

During those five weeks in the *Oronsay*, however, there was pleasure as well as pain. At intervals we drank beer and gin, oozed gentle sweat, played cards and housey-housey, which is now called Bingo, and leant on the rails and watched the porpoises racing and leaping under the bows.

We had a thousand men on board and one girl. She was

a nursing sister, employed in the sick bay, and it was extra-ordinary, in the course of that voyage, how many healthy soldiers found themselves in need of medical care.

She was small and dark, with a sudden smile; but to nine hundred and ninety-nine of us she remained somehow intangible, like the warmth of beauty in a picture. Only one man in the ship could make the picture come alive. He was the first mate, lean, sometimes aloof, always careful of discipline.

We watched them on off-duty hours walking the bridge deck, obviously so happy together that even the most disillusioned old Major among us was inclined to be happy, too.

Once, as we approached the Cape, a fierce argument exploded at a well-deck meeting of Fusiliers—and I may say that when Fusiliers argued the vigour and range of their language would have made Kenneth Tynan on the television sound like an amateur. Then they looked up and saw the girl and the mate at the rail above, hand in hand, looking down at them. The language sputtered out: passion and bad temper subsided. Sheepishly the Fusiliers waved and smiled. One of them tried a friendly wolf-whistle. The girl and the mate laughed and waved back, and for a time life seemed wonderfully pleasant.

The story didn't end there, though it took us some time to catch up with the sequel. Having left us on Madagascar, the *Oronsay* was returning empty to the United Kingdom when a torpedo struck her and she sank, a few miles off the West Coast of Africa. We read in a South African newspaper how the mate had supported our nursing sister in the sea until both were rescued. We read further about their marriage in England.

Some of our 'with it' critics might call this story a barrel of corn, unlikely, unreal, untrue to life. But it happened, exactly as I have told it. Later on we saw death in Madagascar and heard men screaming with festering wounds and sobbing with malaria and dysentery and venereal disease, which, I suppose, is the kind of story a 'with it' critic would approve.

The bitter memories are real enough; but they are supportable because a happy memory of love is also real, and perhaps more enduring.

Our training went on; and finally, a few days out of Durban, we were given the 'pukkah gen'. The Vichy French had control of Madagascar. Churchill, therefore, had decided we ought to move in before the Japanese did and had named the naval base of Diego Suarez in the northern tip as our main objective.

We were provided with maps of the landing-beaches and of the country behind them. Little books were distributed among us giving interesting information about the island itself. They ventured the happy forecast that we should be untroubled by mosquitos or malaria.

Madagascar, it appeared, was the fifth largest island in the world, a patchwork of jungle and desert. A thousand miles long and two hundred and thirty broad, it had about six and a half million inhabitants and from 1895 had been a French protectorate. Its native population was the result of a mixture of races, Malays, Arabs and South Sea Islanders, with elements of French and Negro blood. Though officially Christian, the various tribes were highly superstitious and obsessed by the spirits of the dead.

Its vegetation was lush and in some cases rather odd. The Travellers' Tree, for example, stored water in its leaves, while the pitcher-plant, the legendary Man-eating Tree of Madagascar, had a sticky, poisonous liquid in its vase-shaped pink flowers and could capture and absorb any unfortunate insect venturing too close.

Its animals were equally strange. A few of them, according to our little books, were evolutionary survivors from fifty million years ago. We looked forward to seeing them: the crocodiles, the tailless tandrakas, hairy creatures about the size of a rabbit, and the monkey tribe called lemurs, which included the idris, Marco Polo's Dog-headed Man.

Above all, we looked forward to our first sight of a chameleon. As the gen about chameleons was that they were experts at camouflage and could change colour according to their background, 'Jaggy Feet' began to giggle at the prospect of trying one out on a piece of tartan.

On Thursday, 5 May, the *Oronsay* anchored off Mangoky beach. My platoon began climbing down the scramble-nets into an LCA.

My job was to see the men installed, then to walk round the gunwale and take my place like a Viking chief in the dragon prow. It sounds simple, and so it had been on a diagram chalked on the ship's deck. But now, festooned as I was with weapons and ammunition and compo-rations, and with the LCA dancing a Highland Schottishe in the rough water, the plan soon became unstuck. Half-way round the gunwale I slipped. With a noise like a pot-stand collapsing in an ironmonger's shop, I fell flat on my face in the bottom of the boat.

Sergeant Hibbert picked me up, and the men forgot about a Vichy plane which was half-heartedly machine-gunning the beach. They laughed and went on laughing. And I was glad. In the ship there had existed between officers and men a barrier of Army etiquette and discipline. Now this barrier was broken, and from then on it was a different war as far as I was concerned.

When we got ashore—by which time, thankfully, the Vichy plane had disappeared—I found it was a different war as far as many things were concerned. The maps proved to bear little resemblance to the actual terrain: I found my way by guess and by God—and by Sergeant Hibbert. And despite the optimistic forecasts we were at once attacked by squadrons of muscular mosquitos, with the result that in the next few weeks almost a third of the battalion went down with malaria.

Meanwhile, however, we set out to march the eighteen miles to Antsirane, which lies across the harbour from

F

Diego Suarez. After the cramped and cushioned life in the ship we found it hard to cope with the heat and the dust—and with the sight of blood when our advance elements encountered resistance. On the way we saw none of the fabulous Man-eating Trees or Dog-headed Men we had read about. But we did hear monkeys squalling in the jungle. We did see crocodile snouts in the muddy rivers and smelt the cloying scents of the tropics, which made us remember the peat-smoke and the wet grass at home.

My best memory of that march, however, is of nothing exotic. It is of lying exhausted during a roadside halt, with the sun skinning my face, and 'Jaggy Feet', ignoring his bunions and still with enough energy to brew up, handing me the finest mug of tea I have ever tasted. 'Keep yer chin up, sir! It'll be poorin' wi' rain at the Mull o' Kintyre!'

Madagascar made me decide that if I proved lucky and eventually got back to Southend at the Mull of Kintyre I would never leave it again, wet or dry.

When the fighting was over, we settled down with the mosquitos and the dysentery—and with the scorpions, a new and unexpected hazard for those of us who tried to sleep with our boots off.

Each morning, before dawn, I led my platoon on a recce in our bren-gun carriers, those mini-tanks which could plough through rivers and scrub and climb almost anything except the side of a house. Our brief was to patrol the coast and look out for marauding Japs. We saw no Japs; but on one of those occasions 'Jaggy Feet' was able to satisfy his curiosity about what a chameleon does when placed on a piece of tartan. In fact, nothing spectacular happens. McClymont's specimen did change colour a little, from a sickly brown to a sad shade of green; then it appeared to give up trying, and he called it 'a useless wee bugger'.

Our most interesting find was a village in the forest. Ivovona consisted of a dozen or so round huts made of bamboo and mud. The floor of each hut was raised about a foot from the ground and carpeted with rushes. In one corner was the cooking fire. There was no chimney, however, no exit for the smoke except a rabbit-hutch door, and we could well understand why the Malagasy word for old age means, literally, 'black with soot'.

The men of Ivovona were lean and tall, with light-coloured complexions like Arabs. The women were slim and very straight, even the older ones, though to 'Jaggy Feet' they were as disappointing as the chameleons: 'No' a patch on the Ayrshire lassies!' Their hair-do's were elaborate, braids and plaits plastered high on their heads with castor-oil.

On our way back from patrol we often used to stop outside the village. The Chief was an elderly man with a narrow, lined face and iron-grey hair. His thick lips were sometimes stained red by a vegetable mixture he was in the habit of chewing. He and I would meet under the palm trees, shake hands and sit down, cross-legged, opposite each other. Then his sub-chiefs would approach, bow ceremoniously and squat behind him in a semi-circle, while my NCOs, entering into the spirit of the thing, bowed in their turn and took their places behind me. The other Fusiliers, including 'Jaggy Feet', would stand some distance away and make speculative gestures to the Ivovona ladies giggling and peering out from the huts.

The Chief and I conducted our parleys in French. Neither of us spoke good French, but it was surprising how well we understood each other.

His first invariable act was to rummage beneath his rather off-white robe, or *lamba,* and produce a silver watch, which he told me had been presented to him by a Dutch ship's captain in Zanzibar in 1898. (What he was doing in Zanzibar in 1898 I never found out.) He would ask, *'Quel heure est-il?'* I would tell him, and solemnly he'd move the hands of his watch to the correct time. The watch didn't go—it probably never had done—but this was an unimportant detail.

Then we'd bargain for eggs and chickens in return for cigarettes and compo-rations; and afterwards, with the insects chorussing in the forest, we'd discuss everything from the war to the best way of roasting a sucking pig.

Madagascar has been a completely independent republic since 1960, but one happy result of French influence remains: this total absence of racial self-consciousness that we found in 1942.

I think the Chief must have had a lot in common with old Angus, my great-grandfather in North Uist. He loved leisurely talk. He was a saturated sponge of information about his neighbours and his native island. He was full of the most gruesome superstitions, yet claimed earnestly that he was a Christian.

Like my great-grandfather he had a proverb for all occasions. When warning us about contaminated water in the rivers he reminded us that 'a whole pailful of water is no match for a drop of dirty water'. The first day we met I tried to explain how I envied him the hidden quiet of his forest. He shrugged and smiled. 'No one is ever hidden,' he said. 'Not even in a lonely valley. Zanahary is overhead. Looking down from on high, He sees what is hidden.'

The Chief told us that the original inhabitants of Madagascar were the Vazimba, a race of dwarfs: I wonder if they were Bantus from Africa? Then other tribes came, from Arabia, Persia, India and the South Seas. This was why the Malagasy varied in colour from light brown to jet black.

He spoke reverently about the Vazimba, whose prehistoric stone tombs we sometimes discovered on the hilltops. Indeed, despite his vaunted Christianity, he held the spirits of his dead ancestors in considerable awe. I feel sure he had a witch-doctor hidden away in one of the huts, like a bottle of whisky in a teetotaler's house, in case of emergency.

With a self-conscious and half-credulous grin he told us that evil spirits were partial to children, especially children petted and pampered by their parents. In order that the spirits might believe them to be hated rather than loved and

so leave them unharmed, parents often called their unfor-
tunate offspring by the ugliest names they could think of:
'Manure Heap', for example, or 'Pig Face' or 'Mr Bad
Crocodile'.

In North Uist, Thursday is supposed to be a lucky day to
be born on, because St Columba was born on a Thursday.
In Madagascar the reverse applies: Thursday's children are
considered ill-starred and dangerous. At one time they were
killed at birth.

The Chief had an extraordinary story about an old man
in a neighbouring village whose name was Trabonjy. He
had been born on a Thursday and the same day buried alive
in an ant-heap. A young Christian couple of the same tribe,
suspecting that this might happen, had followed the mother
into the forest. As soon as her back was turned, they had
run forward and rescued the baby, afterwards bringing him
up as one of their own. He had been christened Trabonjy,
which means 'overtaken by salvation'.

The people of Ivovona were innocent and trusting. We
fell in love with them. It makes me sad to think that in the
end we repaid their trust with sacrilege.

Our Brigade Headquarters in Madagascar could have offered
a few wrinkles even to Scotland Yard. In the event of
trouble from the Japs they planned to warn us by transmit-
ting a code word: 'Cromwell' for 'Invasion expected',
'Wolsley' for 'Invasion imminent'.

One night, as I slumbered on a ground sheet at Battalion
HQ, a signaller shook me awake. 'Look, sir! Look what's
come from Brigade!'

I blinked twice at the word on the flimsy. Then I rushed
to the CO in the neighbouring tent.

He read the stark message by the light of a torch, balan-
cing on one hairy leg in his shirt tail. 'Wolsley!' he screamed.
'The Japs are landing! MacVicar, sound the alarm!'

Shades of Omdurman! I got the bugler cracking and then
joined my platoon. Our special duty was to get to the inva-

sion beach as quickly as possible in our bren-gun carriers,
so that we could send back information on the radio.

Still playing General Gordon, the CO came and shook me
by the hand. 'Goodbye, MacVicar. Remember, there will be
no retreat!'

At my back 'Jaggy Feet' was using words under his
breath which reminded me of his original references to
Operation Snowdrop; but I said 'Yes, sir!' with false enthusiasm and mounted my carrier.

We sped off, trying not to think too much about post-
humous VCs.

I wish I could now write about a great battle we fought
against the Japs. The truth is we never saw or heard a sign
of invasion. We spent the night among the sand-dunes sending back 'nothing to report' messages, while 'Jaggy Feet'
brewed up gallons of strong black tea.

The usual anti-climax. Definitely non-Omdurman.

Long afterwards I discovered why the alarm had been
raised. A Japanese two-man submarine had entered the harbour of Diego Suarez. The *Ramillies* had been struck by a
torpedo and damaged so extensively that she was put out of
action for several months. Churchill described the incident
in his book *The Hinge of Fate*.

But for us the real regret of that night had nothing to do
with the tactics and strategy of war. Next morning, on our
way back to Battalion HQ we saw what we had done. In our
mad rush for the beach the night before I had led the
carriers straight through a Malagasy burying-place: the
ancestral burying-place of our old friend, the Chief of Ivovona. The carrier-tracks had torn up the dry earth and
scattered many of the bodies.

We tried to excuse ourselves. It had been dark, the burial-
place was on an open hillside and the shelf-like graves were
not marked in any way. But each of us knew how we should
have felt had invaders violated our own churchyard at
home.

We meant to visit Ivovona and try to express our humble

sorrow; but the opportunity never came. Before it was time for our next patrol we were ordered to leave Madagascar. The Ironclad Snowdrop began in a physical shambles. It ended for us in a kind of moral shambles, which was worse. I am not sure if the Chief would have forgiven us. I wish I could be sure. But after a war, as at the beginning of a war, one is never sure of anything. One can well understand the confusion of a chameleon when confronted with a piece of tartan.

14

If Laughter Comes, Can Tears be far Behind?

FROM Madagascar, with the Fifth Division, we went to India, then to Persia—to a place called Qum above the snowline—and eventually to Sicily and Italy. The war continued to provide boredom, laughter and tears.

The memories of it which most readily come back are those which cause a smile. The other day, on Loch Lomondside near Glasgow, I was caught in a traffic jam. A furniture van lay in a ditch, a fish lorry had its front wheels jammed against a wall, and 'those behind cried "Forward!" and those before cried "Back!" ' My temper has nothing in common with Horatian dignity. But as I sat there fuming in the car I remembered another traffic jam, on a dark mountainside in Italy, and forgot to be angry.

One morning, as we paused near the hilltop village of St Angelo during our long struggle up the Italian spine, Adam MacFarlan, the Adjutant, informed me that for the next few days of my title of MTO was going to read not 'Mechanical Transport Officer' but 'Mule Transport Officer'. Thoughts of jeeps and fifteen-hundredweight trucks, he told me, must immediately be put aside in favour of a villainous looking mob of mules and an equally villainous looking mob of Cypriot muleteers. The battalion, he explained, along with the Seaforths, had been ordered to capture a fairy-tale peak in the near distance and by 2300 hours that very night ought to be dug in on its objective and be thinking about food and drink and cigarettes. As usual, mules or no mules, it was the duty of the MT Section under my command to deliver the goods on time.

When my drivers heard what we had to do their immediate reaction was mutinous. In the end, however, discipline prevailed, and, while the battalion was advancing on its mountain, we spent the afternoon trying to come to terms with our mules and muleteers.

The mules obviously hated the sight of us. The Cypriots had no English except the most obscene swear-words, and my drivers from Ayrshire and Glasgow were only too willing to demonstrate that they, too, were experts in the same linguistic area. Between everything, the future looked far from promising.

It began to get dark. The rain came down, and we were mud to the eyebrows. (Anyone who talks about 'Sunny Italy' has obviously never been there in winter, or else he is an incurable romantic.) Then, in the distance, we heard small-arms fire among the invisible hills. Realising that the battalion had gone into action, we reminded ourselves that their situation was far more dangerous than ours and probably even more uncomfortable. This boosted our flagging morale, and at last the mules were loaded with metal containers of hot food and tea and supplies of various 'comforts'. The colour sergeants arranged them into a straggling column.

When the time came I said, 'Start up!' But of course the mules refused to start, and I thought sadly of the smooth purr of an internal combustion engine and the friendly, antiseptic smell of petrol. (The smell of an uninhibited mule is anything but antiseptic.) The Scottish soldier, however, as I ought to have known, is always equal to the most bizarre occasion. One of my senior drivers, Fusilier 'Ought-Six' Kane, had been taught many curious lessons on the North West Frontier of India, and now, while I stood helplessly wondering what to do next, he opened his clasp-knife and stuck it into the hindquarters of the leading animal. The Italian darkness was filled by a mulish scream of protest, but to my relief the train surged into motion.

The terrain was as dark and as slippery and wet as a peat-hag at the Mull of Kintyre. Being a poor map-reader even in daylight, I had difficulty in following the route, which led higher and higher along a series of vague mountain paths. Several times it occurred to me that we were lost and about to be attacked by a contemptuous and probably ribald enemy. Behind me a continuous groaning, cursing, squealing and clanking did nothing to help my peace of mind.

We had been going for about an hour when it suddenly came to me that we must be on the right track after all. We met the Seaforths, with their mules, coming in the opposite direction.

The meeting, however, occurred at a most awkward place, the middle of a path high in the side of a ravine. (The ravine reminded me irresistibly of the big gorge in Glen Nevis.) The path measured scarcely more than two yards wide. On our left was a sloping drop of some hundred feet, on our right a perpendicular cliff.

For reasons of prestige neither the Fusiliers nor the Seaforths were prepared to give way. We proceeded, therefore, to try and pass each other on that six-foot path. Like Hasdrubal and Hannibal, the Seaforth MTO and I stood aside on a rock to await the outcome.

By this time the rain-clouds had passed over, and in the starlight the scene was indescribable. The language certainly was. Metal containers rang like church bells, rival muleteers yelled at each other in outlandish tongues, mules took bites out of each other, and Lowland swear-words mingled with rich oaths in the Gaelic. Every German within miles must have heard us. One mule fell into the ravine, shrieking as it fell, but sounds coming from below assured me that it was still alive and vigorous. So, as it belonged to the Seaforths, I found no cause to grieve.

Dante's *Inferno* could have been no more hair-raising than this. The chaos went on for hours, or so it seemed. But even the most terrible situation always resolves itself, and at last, thanks mainly to 'Ought-Six' Kane's clasp knife and the sight of his fiendish face in the starlight, the two columns were disentangled and I said a thankful farewell to the Seaforth MTO.

As we neared the battalion position shells began to fall around us. This was no surprise, in view of the noise we were making. I told the Cypriot muleteers to take shelter under a cliff and await our return. They almost wept with gratitude, for by now they were certainly due a break from the mules and the mountaineering and 'Ought-Six' Kane.

A few minutes later, just as the German gunners got our range, we came to a shallow ditch, about seven feet wide, and this the mules refused to cross. It was a moment not of truth but decidedly grim.

But this time the mules themselves resolved the problem, or at any rate one of them did. Nicked by a piece of shrapnel, it took one wild leap into the air and landed in the ditch, where it lay on its side in a sulky but rather comfortable attitude. One of the colour sergeants seized the opportunity. Using the reclining mule as a kind of bridge, by slow degrees he led all the others across it. Then, after much heaving and sweating—and, of course, swearing—we got the unfortunate animal out of the ditch and continued on our way.

Soon afterwards the shelling stopped. We made contact with the battalion on the mountain-top, only to be greeted with glumness and even abuse. The food, it seemed, was scarce. The tea was cold, the cigarettes were lousy. We had arrived very much behind time, and altogether—even with mules—it seemed we had done nothing at all to enhance the reputation of the MT Section.

At this time our CO was Lieutenant-Colonel I. D. McInnes, a regular soldier who had taken over the battalion in Northern Ireland a few months before we sailed for Madagascar. Tall and angular, he had sharp, anxious eyes that looked everywhere. Our previous Colonel had been a 'cushy number'. Our new one was anything but cushy.

The men christened him 'Old Shufti', 'Old' because he had reached the advanced age of thirty-nine and 'Shufti' because this is a Hindustani word meaning 'a close look'—and Colonel McInnes was taking a very close look at us indeed. Everything was wrong, our haircuts, our physical condition, our knowledge of the arts of war and, above all, our discipline. In less than a fortnight we hated his guts.

In the ship to Madagascar he kept it up: orders, instructions, niggling regulations, the enervating PT sessions I have already described.

In the mess he seldom if ever relaxed. Our previous Colonel had always used Christian names. Old Shufti glared and snapped surnames at us. If he smiled, we thought, he might crack his face.

After Madagascar we went on marching, training and doing PT, in the heat of India, in the freezing cold of Persia. That craggy, snarling face haunted us everywhere, though we did have to admit that every horrible privation we suffered, he suffered it, too. At this stage he acquired a walking-stick, which he waved at us like a conductor's baton.

Then, on the beaches of Sicily, we took part in our first real battle; and from that moment something happened, to us and to Old Shufti. The value of our fitness and discipline began to dawn on us. We were the Fusil Jocks, and we didn't care who knew it. As for the CO, his eyes were still sharp, but the anxious look had given way to something else —something we could hardly believe—a kind of shy affection.

One night he shattered us by addressing the Commander of C Company by his Christian name, though the effect was somewhat spoilt when he went on to deliver a gruff lecture on the rules of personal hygiene in the field.

That Hogmanay we were resting in a small Italian town near the Sangro. He came to my billet late at night and I thought to myself, *he's always been dead against the drink, but we're both Scots and this is Hogmanay, and perhaps he, too, is feeling a bit lonely.* I produced a bottle, therefore, and offered him a dram. He took it. He said, 'Good New Year—er—Angus!' and swallowed the whisky neat.

I showed him a photo of my wife and six-year-old son. He studied it for a while. 'Like his mother,' he said at last. 'And lucky for him!' he added, bursting into a snarling laugh.

Before long, however, he pulled himself together, issued a few sharp orders for a move the following day, and departed.

Some time later he got a DSO. He paraded the battalion. 'DSO, not mine, yours. Fine battalion. None better.'

Without a prompt from anyone the men cheered him. He looked astonished. Then for the first time in two years he smiled at his troops, and his smile was one of pure pleasure.

In the evening he approached the Adjutant. 'Adam,' he said, 'just discovered something. Know what the men call me?'

Adam braced himself, because in his time he had heard the CO called many things. 'What's that, sir?' he said.

'Call me Old Shufti. Impudent rascals!'

But he was chuckling, which was a great relief to the Adjutant.

Across the Garigliano, not far from the Appian Way, he waved his stick and led the battalion into an attack. And there he fell, with a German bullet in his forehead. But I think he died happy. I think he knew we had seen through him and understood that his harshness and hard training and discipline had not been for his benefit but for ours.

Soon after the death of Old Shufti, the battalion was ordered to move back out of the line, across the Garigliano.

What happened that night remains another vivid memory for me and also, I believe, for Adam MacFarlan, the Adjutant, who is now a minister and the headmaster of St Kentigern's College in Auckland, New Zealand.

Only one Bailey Bridge was available, long and narrow and 'shoogly' (a Scots word meaning unstable), and it was impressed upon us all that whatever happened the crossing had to be accomplished before midnight, because midnight was the time the methodical Germans were in the habit of shelling the bridge.

There is always a great difference, however, between theory and practice. Everybody was tired after weeks in the line and depressed by the loss of Old Shufti. Tempers were quick, positive reactions slow. At ten minutes to twelve a large number of our trucks and men were still on the wrong side of the river.

It was my duty as MTO to cross last, in my jeep, as a kind of sheep-dog rounding up stragglers. It was dark and it was raining; the confusion was considerable. I listened to and returned volleys of obscene language.

I had already sent my jeep-driver on ahead, in a truck; but Adam was still lingering about, making crude remarks, so, in spite of the fact that technically he was my superior officer, I told him for heaven's sake to get a move on as well. But he said quite firmly that he would wait for me and risk my bad driving in the jeep. This was when I knew that Adam was no fair-weather friend.

In the end the battalion was sorted out and on its way; but as the few trucks rumbled off, the hands of my watch showed only a few seconds before midnight.

Finally Adam and I got going, rattling in first gear on to that long bridge, only too well aware that according to precedent it was now exactly time for the German 'stonk'. Cold shivers were short-circuiting in my dorsal muscles.

Like myself, Adam is a minister's son. A quarter of the way across he said: 'Come on then! Sons of the Manse unite! What about *The Lord's my shepherd*?'

'Sure,' I said.

So we began to sing, like a couple of asthmatic ravens; and when we came to the third verse—'Yea, tho' I walk in death's dark vale'—we gave it the full treatment. And it may have been a quirk of psychology, or it may not, but the journey now seemed shorter and less of an ordeal than it

might have done. In fact, the Germans never shelled the
bridge that night at all. As the man said, 'Life is one damned
anti-climax after another!'

But there is no anti-climax about the Twenty-third Psalm.
It has helped me—and Adam and a host of others—through
many a grim situation.

One more incident in the war is stored in my memory-
bank.

In the week after Christmas, 1944, I went on a day's leave
to Jerusalem along with my company commander, Norman
Milne, who is now a star in Glasgow's legal galaxy. We
engaged a guide with an olive face, a shiny suit and perfume
behind his ears, and he talked and talked. We bought picture postcards in the Garden of Gethsemane and coloured
trinkets at each noisy, jostling Stage of the Cross. We smelt
fungus on the Wailing Wall and saw dirt and squalor
beyond the Jaffa Gate.

By the middle of the afternoon we were hot, sticky and
irritable. We stood on a balcony, looking across the valley
at a mound of yellow rock.

'There,' said our guide, 'lies the Hill of Calvary.' He took a
booklet from his pocket. 'If you wish fuller information
would you care to buy this *History of Jerusalem* at half-
price?'

Norman's fastidious nose had been quivering. Now it
quivered even more. 'My friend,' he said to the guide, 'we
have had enough. Jerusalem might—just might—have been
bearable if people like you had paid less attention to history
and a great deal more to sanitation!'

I can laugh at this devastating judgment now, but at the
time I saw no humour in it, only a sour statement of the
truth. I felt stale, angry and out of sorts. We had arrived in
Palestine from the fighting in Italy and would soon be due
to join the fighting in North West Europe. A day or two
before, news had reached me that Kenneth was missing in
Burma.

What were we fighting for? In some ways Christmas in Jerusalem had symbolised our hopes. But now Christmas in Jerusalem represented nothing at all for us, except perhaps an ugly commerce in religion. Norman and I said good-bye to our guide and walked alone, down the hill, to the Scots Kirk.

Inside it was cool and quiet. The brasses were burnished. The pews were of plain, unvarnished wood.

And then I remembered. Somebody had once told me that many of the seats in the Scots Kirk in Jerusalem had been named after churches at home. I began to search and soon I found what I wanted: on the back of one of the seats a tiny brass plate engraved with the name of my own church, ST BLAAN'S, ARGYLL.

I sat down in it. The noise and the smells and the gaudy colours faded. I saw instead a small, red-roofed bungalow close to the sea and beyond it dark rocks and a yellow strand, where a group of red-shanked black and white oyster catchers stood at the edge of the tide. I saw a frosty glen and in the heart of it a plain, white-washed kirk, with people going in for a Carol Service. I could almost smell the peat-smoke coming from the vestry chimney.

Norman shook me and said: 'I'm not happy about the Latin inscription on the altar. Come and tell me what you think.'

I cared nothing for his Latin inscription, but I went with him and began a happy argument. No longer did I feel stale, angry and out of sorts. Suddenly I knew what we were fighting for, in Jerusalem or anywhere.

That night, back with the battalion, I learnt that Kenneth's wiry, sprinter's legs had proved useful, that he had dodged the Japanese in the jungle and was safe.

It was a good Christmas after all.

As a family after the war we were happy for a time, even though Archie was absent. Then laughter turned to tears again, on account of Rona.

My sister was a golden blonde, with a clear and beautiful complexion. As a teenager she had been inclined to chubbiness, but now she was smart and trim, a revelation to her war-roughened brothers.

Her ambition while at Esdaile School had been to play lacrosse for Scotland. The rest of us were all footballers and athletes of one sort or another, and I think her idea was to 'show us'. She did play once in an international trial, but then the war came and put an end to lacrosse.

She became a teacher at Campbeltown Grammar School and lived at the Manse in Southend with our parents and Maimie and John, who was still at school. She had the same quiet sense of humour as my mother, and the pair of them usually kept the more extrovert male members of the family in their places.

I cannot say if Rona was ever in love. Some believe that she was—during the war while we were away—and that the ending was unhappy. She never spoke about it to me, and in any case it made no difference to the warmth in her eyes or to the affection she showed her friends.

Her new ambition was to become a singer of Gaelic songs, for she had discovered a talent for music. And when Rona set her mind to anything, she never gave up without good cause. She took singing lessons and Gaelic lessons, her target being a Gold Medal at the annual Gaelic Mod, the Scottish equivalent of the Welsh Eisteddfod.

Some time before the Mod in 1948, she had a small operation and afterwards was subject to huskiness, which was worrying for her as a singer. I was worried, too, by how thin she was becoming but put it down to hard work at school and in her preparation for the Mod.

Then the doctor told me. Rona had cancer, and there was no cure. Soon her voice would leave her.

Though the doctor shared his knowledge only with me, I am sure that she herself suspected the truth; but her mood remained happy as the date of the Mod came closer.

With four days to go she took another sore throat and

became so husky that singing was impossible. She must have been bitterly disappointed; but she set off for Glasgow, determined at any rate to enjoy the fun at the great Gaelic Festival.

The night before the opening of the Mod her huskiness left her, completely. Her throat was still painful, but she could sing. And sing she did in St Andrew's Hall, where with two of the loveliest Gaelic songs I know, *Dream Angus* and *When I was Young,* she won her Gold Medal by a wide margin. Next day the newspapers called her 'The Girl with the Golden Voice'.

Not long afterwards her voice left her again. This time it didn't come back. She died the following year, still gay and full of humour, and I am glad to remember that most of the sadness was in us and not in her.

15

An Author in Scotland

BACK in Southend after the war, precariously financed by a gratuity of £400, I took a cool look at the situation. Encouraged by Jean—and by the family—I decided to start writing again. It was a worrying decision but perhaps inevitable. In his *Authors and the Book Trade* Frank Swinnerton writes:

'Although authorship is the hardest work above ground, although its rewards have always a sting and its failures very few consolations, although fame soon loses its charm and may involve the complete sacrifice of privacy, although no day passes without its bitter humiliation, the writer, once stung, is as one hypnotised. Despairing of his own talent, completely in the dark as to the virtue or otherwise of what he has spun from his imagination, he gropes onward to even deeper darkness, accompanied by the candid criticisms of his friends and juniors, who tell him that he would be better dead. . . . Having read (and believed) the depressive truths I have communicated, do you still wish to become a writer? Do you still prefer the hideous mischances of authorship to the safe, comfortable and prosperous occupations of the miner, the airman, the racing motorist, the soldier, the statesman, the steeplejack, the nurse, the charwoman, or the housebreaker? Then you are born to authorship as the sparks fly upward.'

Frank Swinnerton, that wise and kindly doyen of our craft, has never written truer words. I don't think I could have been happy in any profession other than authorship.

Since 1945, in the front room at Achnamara overlooking

the bay and the dark rock of Dunaverty, I have written many books, more than half of them for children, at least five hundred scripts for radio and television, scores of newspaper serials, short stories and one-act plays—and even picture by picture instructions for strip cartoons. Dull moments are few, and Jean is liberal with cups of tea. I am also fortunate in having a clever lady from Hull who types my scripts, rules my punctuation and spelling with an iron hand and tells me that my handwriting is worse than the Padre's.

When I enter the clubhouse at Dunaverty golf course I am sometimes greeted by the steward, Duncan Watson, with the remark: 'Here he comes, the biggest liar in Scotland, and he makes a fortune out of it!' I haven't made a fortune as a writer, and don't expect to do so, simply because under present conditions the economics of authorship are like something out of *Alice in Wonderland*.

From a £1 book, for example, the author gets his ten per cent, which is ten new pence. When this book is bought by a public lending library hundreds of people read it for free, and the author still only gets his ten pence. Musicians, singers —and the Beatles—all receive a royalty each time their records are played in public. But under the present library system an author is expected to provide the public with free entertainment and count himself privileged to do so. Do his readers provide him with free coal, free butter, free newspapers, free typewriters?

For years the Society of Authors has been trying to persuade Parliament to pass a Public Lending Rights Bill, which would give books the same royalty protection as gramophone records, so far, however, without success. The trouble is, authors are few. Miners and dockers, farmers and shipbuilders are much more numerous and therefore able to make much more noise. There is also the matter of voting power. Once at a public political meeting in Southend, I asked Michael Noble, MP for Argyll, if he would support our Bill for PLR. He knew all the answers to agricultural questions put to him by an audience composed mainly of farmers, but his reply to a lone author was that he had never even heard of a PLR Bill. Only a few years previously, however, according to the records, he voted against Sir A. P. Herbert's original attempt to introduce one.

Scarcely anybody today can live by writing books and nothing else. A freelance author has to find other markets for his storytelling. As I struggled to regain my feet after the war I was lucky to find one such market in radio and television. My luck was due, in the first instance, to a lady now retired from the BBC, Kathleen Garscadden of Children's Hour.

An author is a sensitive kind of creature, full of confidence one minute, stiff with depression the next. Kathleen knew exactly how to deal with him. She was a hard taskmistress, but she knew what she wanted, and because her writers felt that in spite of everything she was sympathetically aware of their difficulties and fears, they worked like navvies for her.

She had a genius for spotting up-and-coming young actors, and many whose names are now famous were helped and encouraged by her. One of Stanley Baxter's first acting engagements was in a radio serial I wrote in 1950 called *Faraway Island*. In those days he was an earnest adolescent but obviously destined to go places. Rikki Fulton was also one of Kathleen's 'juvenile leads' and played Stubby, a schoolboy character of mine. Gordon Jackson and Rona Anderson became engaged while working together in one of our serials—*King Abbie's Adventure*—and I can remember the afternoon when Kathleen made frantic signs to me to stop being stupid and to leave them alone in the studio while the rest of us went for a break to the canteen.

There are many others still in the BBC, of course, without whose good will my job as an 'electronic' storyteller would be impossible. When I sit talking in a television studio I am surrounded by people metaphorically holding my nervous hand: producers, secretaries, vision-mixers, studio and floor

managers, cameramen, sound men, lighting experts, caption
operators, autocue operators and engineers of every variety
and description. I depend on them all. They depend on each
other, and in a way—heaven help them!—they also depend
on me. It is like being in a war again.

In more than a quarter of a century of working as a freelance at Broadcasting House in Glasgow I have always been
given the utmost courtesy and kindness by every member of
the staff, from the mightiest producer down through the
echelons of artists and technicians to the charming recep-
tionists, commissionaires and cloakroom attendants. Many
of them I count my closest friends.

It is an odd fact, however, that in all those twenty-five
years I have never once spoken to—or, as far as I am aware,
even seen—a Scottish Controller or Head of Programmes. I
have a mental picture of those two gentlemen, white-robed
and holy, ensconced on fat and comfortable clouds above
Broadcasting House, peering down with aloof disfavour on
the antics of its inmates. The picture is influenced, perhaps,
by an etching in the Padre's big family Bible. It depicts
Abraham and Moses, enthroned in a cloud-cuckoo heaven,
frowning down upon a seething, troubled world.

It was Kathleen Garscadden who encouraged me to start
writing for children. I am glad I took her advice.

As far as I can make out, there is no particular *mystique*
about writing for children, except that one must be able to
tell a gripping story in clear and unambiguous language—
which, of course, is a good recipe for adult books as well.
Stories by John Buchan, Hammond Innes and Arthur
Clarke, for example, not written specifically for young
readers, are as popular with children as with adults.

Several of my own children's books have been serialised
in adult publications, while, astonishingly, one of my adult
books, *Escort to Adventure,* was serialised in a children's
magazine in Holland. One answer to this may be that I have
a good agent. Another may be that I have a reasonably

straightforward and simple mind, which I hope is not the same as being simple-minded.

Kathleen always insisted that any story I wrote for her should have what she called 'an ethic'. I was happy to comply. A number of 'with it' writers, mostly self-styled, have canvassed the idea that children dislike a story with a moral. I have never found the slightest evidence of this. If a writer has a philosophy—and every writer worth his salt has some kind of philosophy—I think he has a duty to reveal it. If he does his job with artistry and sincerity, then children will read what he has written. They may reject his ideas, but at any rate they will have been encouraged to think for themselves.

The primary object of a writer for children is surely to entertain. At the same time, what is wrong with suggesting that reverence and respect for one's fellow beings is a good thing, a practical solution to many problems in this hard world?

During the past twenty years children have changed tremendously, as far as their knowledge and 'know-how' is concerned. Modern children read newspapers and watch television. Their outlook is far more sophisticated than mine was at their age. (Than it is now, I sometimes think.) So is their vocabulary. My thirteen-year-old niece Marsali thinks nothing of broaching the subject of abortion at the breakfast-table, much to the concealed embarrassment of both her parents.

Marsali's case is perhaps not typical: she is John's daughter, and John is a gynaecologist. But when one reads about a girl of thirteen becoming engaged, when one reads about a fourteen-year-old boy experimenting with 'pot', one has got to face the fact that children of today—the older ones at any rate—just won't be fobbed off with pumpkin-coaches and 'midnight feasts in the dorm'. Young minds are searching for a proper sense of values, not in relation to a bygone social order but in relation to Vietnam and apartheid, the space race and 'the pill'.

It is no good saying that children ought to be protected from all this dangerous stuff. They don't want to be protected. They want to know the facts and form their own opinions and have their say. I wonder if some of the current adolescent unrest might be traced back to fond parents—and even fonder teachers and writers—trying to wrap their sweet darlings in too much tinsel and cotton-wool?

It seems to me that the duty of those of us who write for children is to try to help in guiding these fresh young minds towards honest and ethical judgments. Basic guidance in this and every other field of welfare ought to be the responsibility of the family unit; but society in general and writers in particular should also be concerned.

Many writers for children do indeed have a social conscience, and this is reflected in the high standard of new children's books published today: books which describe life as it is, not as some fantastic Utopia inhabited only by dream children and the idle rich.

If children have become sophisticated, however, so have children's writers themselves, if only in self-defence. When I wrote the first *Lost Planet* book nearly twenty years ago I got away with only a smattering of scientific knowledge. Now, if I am not to be laughed off the lists, I have to be Arthur Clarke, Werner von Braun and Yuri Gagarin rolled into one. After doing months of research for my new *Super Nova* stories, I feel ready to sit for a B.Sc. (Space), with honours.

At the same time, breathing heavily, I still try to show that the study of science is much less important than the study of humanity. I also do my best to give practical answers to problems of space research still in the balance. And to prevent me becoming pompous about it all, I keep continually in mind a story which the Rev. Kenneth Mac-Leod used to tell. A Highland minister was preaching violently about Hell—'And there shall be weeping and wailing and gnashing of teeth'—when suddenly, in a pew near the pulpit, he spotted an old gentleman with no teeth at all, who was grinning wickedly. But the minister scarcely even paused. 'As for you, my friend,' he said, *'teeth will be provided!'* A practical answer indeed, and one hard to disprove, even by a scientific genius of fourteen.

What then, in a short definition, is a good book for children? I suppose there could be as many answers as there are readers of this book. For myself, applying a similar standard as in the case of adult literature, and taking my cue from what children themselves have written on the subject, I suggest that first and foremost it is entertaining and exciting. It is also real, in the sense that it deals with truth and not, for example, with wealth fantasy or power fantasy. Finally, it is a guide to the emotions and stimulating to the young imagination. It follows, of course, that a book which satisfies all these conditions is also well written.

Authorship is certainly not a life of safe security. I sit down at my desk every morning about half past nine and stop about five o'clock in the afternoon, with no help at all from Government subsidies or Arts Council grants or demarcation systems. Indeed, a freelance author is one of the last survivors of genuine free enterprise. Holidays are expensive and therefore rare; but I try to keep physically fit by taking regular exercise, walking and golfing, and mentally alert by joining in every kind of parish activity, from the holy Church to the 'godless Drama'.

The job, of course, has its advantages. I have independence, something dear to the heart of a Hebridean Scot. I can cock my snook at editors and publishers when I feel inclined, though I admit this doesn't happen often: certainly not when a wolf is howling at the door. In the same way, if I feel like a game of golf in the afternoon I can have one and finish my daily thousand words in the evening instead.

Continually, however, an author must have faith: faith in his own talent and faith in 'a divinity that shapes our ends'. Sometimes mine has been wobbly. In moments of depression, with an overdraft staring me in the face, I have often been tempted to try writing pornographic books, which sell so readily, frequently in the guise of 'literature'. So far I haven't succumbed, and I don't think I will now. For one thing, pornography is such bad art. For another, it must give the writer the kind of sad insecurity experienced by a prostitute, and I should hate hearing people say they were sorry for me.

There is nothing wrong with sex, of course, in books or elsewhere. It is a part of life and a most enjoyable part if approached with love. But I don't think a writer should concentrate on it. There is so much more to life, like love and hate, nobility and treachery, self-sacrifice and selfishness, innocence and hypocrisy.

The great books are balanced, integrated, the mirror of all sides of life. Some day I may write such a book, if and when the Almighty reckons I am fit for it.

From all this high-sounding stuff, from all the mass of personal reminiscence that has gone before, does my philosophy as a writer emerge? I don't know. I keep groping towards truth and never getting there. I keep setting up ideals which have a habit of exploding in my face.

I prefer sentiment to sadism, democracy to dictatorship, warm love to cool calculation. But I myself am often sadistic, dictatorial, calculating. Sometimes I suspect I have a stammer in my logic as well as in my tongue. This being so, have I any right to try to preach, as the Padre did and the old MacVicars?

I am a Scot, with the family pride of a Scot and a good deal of the puritanism of a Scot. Puritanism can be a basis for self-discipline, which is something every professional author must have: I am not ashamed of this streak in my character. But pride?

Let me be humble and use the words of a great Englishman to define the philosophy I should like to reveal in my writing, though it is probable I nearly always fail:

> This above all: to thine own self be true,
> And it must follow, as the night the day,
> Thou canst not then be false to any man.

As I said, I keep setting up ideals. This leads to great happiness and great pain.

Is it worth it?

Of course.

IN MEMORIAM

The Padre

died 26 September, 1970

Index